Life. Be In It.

Words of Wisdom, Humor,
and Encouragement

Other books by Susan A. Marshall:

How to Grow a Backbone:
10 Strategies for Gaining Power and Influence at Work

Forthcoming books by Susan A. Marshall:

Of Beauty and Substance: A Backbone Guide for Women
The Rise of Emerging Leaders: A Backbone Guide
for Young Professionals
Leveraging Your Genius: A Backbone Guide for Geeks
Minding the Social Fabric: A Backbone Guide
for Non-Profit Leaders
Raising the Future: A Backbone Guide for Parents
Empowering the Future: A Backbone Guide for Educators

Life. Be In It.

Words of Wisdom, Humor, and Encouragement

Susan A. Marshall

MAVEN
MARK
BOOKS

Milwaukee, Wisconsin

Published by MavenMark Books,
a division of HenschelHAUS Publishing, Inc.
2625 S. Greeley St. Suite 201
Milwaukee, WI 53207
www.henschelhausbooks.com
Please contact the publisher for permissions or quantity discounts.

ISBN: 978-159598-208-7
Library of Congress Control Number: 212953339

Also available in most e-book formats.

Library of Congress Cataloging-in-Publication Data available on request.

Cover design by EM Graphics.

Printed in the United States of America.

This book is for you, Mom.

In honor of your
incredible strength and resilience
in raising six rowdy kids,
your dedication in caring for Dad
despite your own sorrow and loss,
and for showing me how
to endure life's stormiest days
to fully appreciate the sunny ones.
I love you.

Table of Contents

Preface

We all show up in this world oblivious. We have nothing to our name—and maybe not even a name for a day or two. We cannot speak or make sense of the noise around us. We have no means of satisfying our hunger; indeed we do not know how to operate the many systems that make up our bodies.

Little by little, over a long period of time, we figure things out. Sometimes we have help from family, friends, and various institutions and agencies; sometimes we are not so lucky. Our hearts tell us before we know the words that we want to be seen and heard. We want someone to understand us. We want to be loved. And we know that somehow, someway, some day we will make a difference.

Life unfolds. Straight and narrow paths become long and winding roads in one remarkable journey. Good days make our hearts sing and our minds conjure new adventure. Bad days can leave us wondering what it's all about.

This book is a tribute to life and its unpredictable ways. I've come to appreciate life's surprises, though like most of my friends, I'd rather have the chance to pass on some of the heart-wrenching ones. But I would miss some powerful lessons.

More than that, this book is a tribute to every human who engages in life. Your story is unlike any other, shaped by the push and pull of life; the blows and blisters as well as the comforts and caresses. To those of you who have accomplished great successes and touched countless lives, I thank you for being a role model. To those who have given up, I am sorry you despaired. Another better day was on its way. That's how life is, you know. Every day is unique and unpredictable. We cherish the best ones and tolerate the worst.

I hope this book challenges, encourages, and inspires you to get into your life. Shape it. Make it move. Make it matter. And appreciate everything that happens along the way. It's your turn; it's your time.

Life. Be in it.

Life. Be in it.

Once upon a time, a *long* time ago before I had kids and grandkids, I was walking through Regner Park in West Bend, appreciating the beauty of a late September day. The sky was an incredible shade of blue, the breeze was crisp, and the trees wore spectacular colors. I stopped and stood still on a pathway to drink in the splendor of the day. In that stillness, I noticed a set of rollicking figures painted over the top of the beach house that said "*Life. Be in it.*"

I was struck by the simplicity and cheerfulness of the sign and spent the rest of the day thinking about it. Many years have passed since then and my life has been filled, sometimes to overflowing. But I have never forgotten the expression. Now, nearly four decades later, it is painted over my kitchen sink as a daily reminder and source of encouragement.

"*Life. Be in it.*" What a delightful directive! Think of how different your life could be if you truly got into it.

It is true that life has been especially difficult lately. I, like so many others, have experienced the stress, worry, and outright fear of wondering what will happen if something doesn't change. But I'm still here. You are reading this, so you're still here. Somehow or other, we continue to find our way. This is worth appreciating!

Think back over the days and years of your life so far. Major events often define the ups and downs, the joys and sorrows. But it's the little things that stick in a person's mind. Burnt-out grass and iced-over driveways. The gentle lapping of water along a shoreline, and the rustle of dried leaves in a crisp autumn wind. Broken bones and really bad haircuts. Heartbreaks. Stitches. Butterfly kisses and cartwheels with the kids.

The euphoria of your team winning a close game, and the despair of being on the losing side. The start of the car's engine, and the sound of the door closing as a loved one returns home.

Report cards and the Tooth Fairy. Loud music and muddy floors. Spilled milk and burnt toast. Lost tempers and found forgiveness.

Private gestures of affection—winks, ET finger touches, hugs. Family rituals. Favorite meals. Dreaded conversations. Gut-wrenching setbacks and refusals to give up. Potato chips for lunch, hot coffee or tea at breakfast. Beloved smiles and farewell prayers as caskets close.

Life presents an incredible array of joys and sorrows, giggles and sobs, tests and rewards. And it arrives every morning, whether we are ready for it or not.

So why not welcome it, embrace it, accept it for what it is and show up with curiosity and courage? You have been through tough stuff, maybe a lot of it. You have also been shown many kindnesses, large and small. You have been cared about and cared for. You have had the privilege of caring for others and letting them know how special, how dear, they are to you.

When you think about all the little things that make up your days and the adventures you have already experienced, you start to see that your life *has* mattered. You may begin to realize that you are stronger than you've given yourself credit for. You find a way to appreciate everyone you have encountered, even the annoying ones.

These little moments define real life for the majority of us. They capture the essence. You may struggle to pay your bills, hold on to your job, or maintain your health. Some of these struggles can feel overwhelming and there are days when you honestly don't see a way to keep going. At these times, my brother, Steve, likes to say, "Grab your mitt and get in the game."

I look up as I sip my coffee and remind myself, "*Life. Be in it.*"

Reaching for Greatness

*R*eaching for greatness, contrary to popular lore, does not mean you must be the best, brightest, fastest, most beautiful, brainiest, richest, or first at something in order to be successful in your quest. Rather, it means discovering the gifts that lie within you, doing something to develop them, finding a way to make a contribution, and enjoying the satisfaction that comes from doing something that matters. To you.

> *Never underestimate the power of dreams and the influence of the human spirit. We are all the same in this notion: The potential for greatness lies within each of us.*

So said Wilma Rudolph and she should know. Wilma was the first American woman to win three gold medals in a single Olympics in Rome, 1960. Born prematurely, the 20th of 22 children, and weighing just 4.5 pounds, Wilma's life is a testimony to reaching for greatness against remarkable odds.

A General's Words of Wisdom

*They teach you to be proud and unbending in honest failure,
but humble and gentle in success; not to substitute words for
action; not to seek the path of comfort, but to face the stress
and spur of difficulty and challenge; to learn to stand up in the
storm, but to have compassion on those who fall; to master
yourself before you seek to master others; to have a heart that
is clean, a goal that is high; to learn to laugh, yet never forget
how to weep; to reach into the future, yet never neglect the
past; to be serious, yet never take yourself too seriously; to be
modest so that you will remember the simplicity of true
greatness, the open mind of true wisdom, the meekness of
true strength.*

*T*hese words are taken from General Douglas MacArthur's speech to West Point cadets given in 1962. MacArthur was 82 years old, and during his life, he had seen both a brilliant military career and an awkward recall from duty. MacArthur represents the stereotypical big shot general—bold, arrogant, tough as nails. The

West Point cadet calls to mind another stereotype. Complete with square jaw line, steely eyes, stiff spine, and uncrackable composure, he is the military preppy.

Who can relate to these guys? And what do they have to do with us regular people? Who cares about them and some speech about "duty, honor and country?" After all, patriotism in this sense is not fashionable today.

But read the passage again and you'll see that even these stone-faced military guys think like "normal" people. They want, just as we do, to develop themselves as individuals. They want to be important. They want to be proud of themselves. The ideals are lofty but not unattainable.

The message for us is that it doesn't really matter what you do in life, or whether you are destined for the pages of history books. Rather, it is the rules you play by, the goals you set, and the principles you believe in that make you and your endeavors just as big and just as important as those of General MacArthur or the West Point cadets.

Anticipate Success

The happiest and most successful people are those who set out to do things fully expecting to have their efforts rewarded. They anticipate success. They believe in themselves. They work hard to make things happen. This positive outlook gives them the fire, the spirit, and the vigor they need to get things done.

The anticipation of success is a powerful key to unlocking the energy and creativity that lies within you. The anticipation of success is what causes you to pull off your boots and jump into the mainstream of life; to shoot the rapids with more confidence than fear; and to navigate each new bend eager to discover what lies ahead.

The anticipation of success is what enables you to develop your talents and use them fully, happily and without embarrassment to create a better life for yourself and those you care about.

To anticipate success is to precondition your mind for success. It is an exciting concept that produces dramatic results. But if you are like so many, you may look at the success of others and attribute it to luck or inheritance. You may find it hard to believe that you can make good things happen simply by expecting good results from your focused efforts. But you can.

The next time you call someone to ask for a favor, put a smile on your face and in your voice. Make your request with conviction that it will be granted. Don't worry about getting "no" for an answer; don't even consider the possibility. Be upbeat and positive and you will find others more willing to accommodate you.

Take the same approach the next time you discipline your children. Remove the irritation from your voice and replace it with a lighter, firmer tone that conveys your positive expectation. A corrective message delivered in such a way will be heard more readily than one voiced in anger or frustration. No, this will not necessarily prove easy to do. But by anticipating a successful outcome, you set the stage for favorable results.

Practice with small things in your daily life. Each time you do something, focus on the results you want rather than on the difficulties you might encounter. Learn to anticipate success. Learn to anticipate fun. Before long you will find that you are looking forward to each new day full of zest, full of life.

At What Age Do Dreams Die?

Creativity takes courage. Lots of courage.

Courage to be an individual, unique and unfettered by the *oughts* and *shoulds* of others. Courage to speak uncommon thoughts and dream unheard-of dreams. Courage to rise after falling, smile after setbacks, and hold your head high after taking it on the chin.

Creativity, though much wished for by many, is seldom seriously cultivated. We tend, instead, to carve out ruts and mold our spirits and actions to fit the ruts. Sometimes old patterns chafe, but not enough to force us out of our self-made trenches to peer over the rim into the vast unknown. It's scary out there!

Sometimes we feel an urge to explore and broaden our horizons, but before we drift too far a-sea, we quell our impulsiveness.

Many of us content ourselves with the thought that as we grow older it is only proper to settle down some and put old yearnings to rest in the name of maturity, sensibility and responsibility. But at what age do dreams die? And how do we justify ourselves as we switch from saying, "Maybe I can" to, "If only I had?"

We can cop out, sure. We can resign ourselves to anything. On the other hand, it is also true that whatever we truly set our hearts and minds to, we can accomplish.

You may have heard the story of the old man who, lying in tears on his deathbed said, "I cry not because I am dying, but because I have never lived."

There is no greater tragedy than to allow your creativity—yes, you have it in great quantities—to go wasted and die unused at the end of your life. Start now to dream dreams. It doesn't matter how old you are. Start now to try things, to reach for those goals that deep down you have always wanted to take a shot at. There is no satisfaction, no glory, no legacy in things left undone. There is no joy in looking back and wondering why, with all the time you once had, you attempted so little.

Unleash your creativity. How? Simply be. To the very best of your ability, in all your glory and with all your flaws. Dare to be happy. You'll find that the more freedom you allow yourself, the more creativity will spring to the surface. It is not an elusive quality reserved for only a select few. It is within you. Think of all the great ideas you've had in the shower!

But remember, creativity takes courage. Those ideas will never see the light of day unless you share them. It takes courage to make your unique contribution to the world. Start today. There's no one else who can do what you can do. Share it. Do it. Be it.

Be Inspired, then Get Determined!

*I*nspiration is like the ignition in your car: essential to get started and insufficient on its own to take you where you want to go.

Inspiration comes in all forms; when you become aware of it, you'll find it is everywhere! Some of my favorites include double rainbows, intense thunder storms, a perfectly made veggie omelet, certain types of music, sudden laughter and of course the stories of unlikely success against nearly impossible odds, like Kentucky Derby winner, I'll Have Another.

It feels good to be inspired, especially when inspiration takes you by surprise. A sudden burst of goodness in your life makes you yearn to do the things you know you could if you put your mind to it.

And there's the rub. Who has time to put your mind to a dream that lingers in your heart? When there is nothing spectacularly wrong with your life, it is hard to catapult yourself into something much more exciting. The drip, drip, drip of daily demands can suffocate that spark of inspiration that had you so fired up just a couple of days ago.

If inspiration is ignition, then determination is like the rest of your car's systems—the engine, gears, brakes and everything else under the hood. These systems take you where you want to go, often without your having to think much about it. Determination is what makes dreams come true because it clicks ideas into gear.

Determination involves making a conscious decision to follow through on your excitement by creating a roadmap, putting a system in place to check your progress, and finding little ways to reward yourself as you navigate toward your dream.

Determination doesn't care if your energy level is low today. It doesn't pay any attention to whether other people notice you working hard on your goal. It doesn't check the weather or your horoscope and it doesn't care if you're struggling with a bad hair day.

Determination is about doing what you said you wanted to do. It consists of baby steps taken every day that move you closer to that thing you yearn for. Determination draws on inspiration and deepens it to help you create the life you truly want.

When you lay out a plan to move forward and keep track of the things you do along the way, you create your own inspiration. Watching yourself succeed is one of the surest ways to fuel momentum. Anyone who has ever been on a diet—and who among us hasn't—knows this. When you look outrageously gorgeous for that big party, you feel great. Nobody knows the tedious hours you spent adjusting your foods, working your body, and staying on course. But you do. That's powerful. It is what inspiring stories are made of!

I will admit that determination is tough to hold onto in our hyperactive, always-on world. It's hard to ignore the onslaught of new information coming at you from all directions. It is difficult to purposely ignore things that have no bearing on your goal—who likes to feel uninformed? It is also difficult to turn down an invitation to hang out with friends or attend a meeting that might hold something of value.

All these distractions form innocent little cracks through which determination seeps away. When it is gone, you feel sad. Disappointed. Maybe angry with yourself for not following through on your plan.

Here's an invisible truth about life. Every day you amass evidence that tells you something about yourself. This evidence—from promises kept or broken to how you perform, impressions you create, and things you accomplish—will cause you to give yourself a thumb's up, a shrug, or a sad shake of the head. Think about that for a minute. Why wouldn't you find as many ways as you can to create positive evidence of your capability and accomplishment?

Take time to be purposely inspired, then capture that energy with a plan to fuel your determination. And don't forget to pause once in a while to celebrate what you have already achieved. You are one inspiring human.

Doing Business Your Way

*E*ntrepreneurs are the darlings of the business media; have been for a couple of decades now. They used to be a rare breed, but the explosion of technologies, an expanding global marketplace, and a sea of willing investors now offer rich and continuing financial rewards for people who can envision and execute a new and useful idea.

An entrepreneur, broadly defined, is someone who seeks to capitalize on new and profitable endeavors or business, usually with considerable initiative and risk. An entrepreneur seeks to build an enterprise and in doing so, sets herself apart from the independent contractor or free agent who seeks to make a living—and sometimes a fortune—doing her work.

Where do they come from?

The 2007 Global Entrepreneurship Monitor, an annual assessment conducted by London Business School and Babson College, offered these key findings:

- Many low-income countries are exhibiting high rates of early-stage entrepreneurial activity. The top three hot-spots for early stage entrepreneurship are Thailand, Peru and

Columbia. The lowest activity was in Russia, Romania, and Latvia.

♦ Among high-income countries, Iceland, Hong Kong and the United States lead the way; the lowest activity was found in Austria, Puerto Rico and Belgium.

♦ In Latin America and the Caribbean, gender differences are relatively small. In high-income countries, men are about twice as likely as women to be involved in early-stage entrepreneurial activity.

Why do they do it?

The most popular stories involve the talented souls who get fed up with bureaucracy and rote, chuck their corporate titles and chart a new course with bold confidence. Kind of like Dilbert turned Richard Branson. Or maybe their less famous sisters.

Certainly, that's the case for some. But the deeper reasons people start their own companies are to execute a better way, to bring a better idea to market, to espouse particular values and to devote their time and talents to making some sort of difference in the world.

It's a complicated venture that involves knowledge of many types, a team of trusted colleagues and advisors, and mental and physical stamina that borders on Herculean. Because of this, it is wise to study a business idea keenly even if quickly, before jumping into the fray. And have profit as a stated intention.

Must you be an entrepreneur to have the freedom to do business your way? The answer depends on your definition of freedom. If freedom means trusting your view of the world above all others and wishing to make final calls based on this view, then the answer is probably yes. If it means challenging yourself to the limits of your capability and being willing to own the outcome, the answer is yes again. If you want your name on the building, it's the only way aside from inheriting a family enterprise. As an entrepreneur, you will still seek the counsel of others and you will need to be able to share your vision in a way that gets people on board and excited about building what you see. The best promise of entrepreneurialism is that bright, motivated people really can change the world with what they create.

But this can happen in an existing business as well. Successful turnarounds come at the hands of skillful people, adept at deciphering market opportunity and aligning people and systems to capitalize on it.

As for the deeper reasons people start their own companies, I've long thought that it's possible to change any situation—to improve processes, incubate ideas, live personal values and make a difference— wherever you are. Some would argue that starting a company provides the opportunity to put these in place from the very beginning. That's true. But the struggle for resources, particularly in early stage development, can make these ideals more high-minded than practical.

The bottom line on entrepreneurship is that there is more opportunity than ever before to create the company of your dreams. With careful research, adequate funding, a willingness to shoulder risk and the determination to never look back, you can be well on your way.

Which brings me to an apparent paradox of entrepreneurialism. It's not as simple as it sometimes appears and almost anyone with a keen idea and an undeterred will to win can succeed. Just look at what happened at Google.

Free To Be...Thee!

$\mathcal{I}$ love the 4th of July in Wisconsin with its parades and picnics, flags and fireworks and brimming good feelings of strength and pride and freedom. Happy Independence, Wisconsin women!

What? You're not excited about this holiday? You don't do parades or picnics?

Alas, too many women today feel somewhat less than jubilant this 4th of July. Economic conditions have increased their feelings of vulnerability, stress, and worry.

What's free, after all, about the pressures of job, home, relationships, or families?

Your choice, that's what. I know this sounds simple-minded and may not seem relevant to your current circumstances, but it is critically important to recognize that you do have choices. Lots of them.

The first begins with the way you think about challenge. Who is the boss of your life? You are, of course. You may feel strong influences from your boss at work, your spouse or significant other, even your kids and their demands. But you are the only one who decides how to invest your time each day. You are the only one who controls what goes into your head and stays there. You are the only one who sees life through your eyes and knows what you wish it to be.

In that regard, you are in the very same place as those who influence you so strongly. You influence them, too! I often wonder what life would be like if we could share what we see and what we want in a spirit of curiosity and wonder, rather than with the often unspoken demands or expectations we place on one another?

You can change this particular aspect of your life, starting right now. It's not easy and it won't be quick, but the first step is sorting out for yourself where you are, where you want to go, and how you want your life to be each day. Think about the things you do that make you feel happy and strong. Write them down and do more of them!

Some women love to get up with the sun to go for a walk or run. They feel strong and energized afterwards. Others like to make lists before going to bed or with their first cup of coffee or tea in the morning. This helps them feel organized and purposeful. Some like to read and meditate each day for the feelings of serenity and acceptance it brings. Still others love to interact with kids, neighbors, or friends because it reminds them that we're all in this together.

Whatever makes you feel healthy and strong and whole, do it! Then share your good feelings with the people you love. Don't expect them to do what you do or even to change their behavior one way or another. Just share your happiness. You'll find that it eases a lot of tension!

As you feel more grounded, think logically through your issues. What is going on and who is involved? What would you like to change about the situation? Remember, you can only change you! Bring your best self to each situation and do what makes you proud. Forgive mistakes, both yours and others. Don't sweat the small stuff!

Despite some very challenging circumstances this 4th of July, please remember that you are free to be yourself. Dream a little. Work on what matters. Smile at yourself when you accomplish even small goals. You're creating your life one day at a time. Make it worth your best effort!

In celebration of independence, here are some words of inspiration by women who understood freedom.

Believe in yourself. You gain strength, courage, and confidence by every experience in which you stop to look fear in the face. You must do that which you think you cannot do.

—Eleanor Roosevelt

Character cannot be developed in ease and quiet. Only through experience of trial and suffering can the soul be strengthened, ambition inspired, and success achieved.

—Helen Keller

Whatever my individual desires were to be free, I was not alone. There were many others who felt the same way.

— Rosa Parks

All great achievements require time. If you don't like something, change it. If you can't change it, change your attitude.

—Maya Angelou

From Stuck to Stoked: A Formula for Change

*S*tories of stuck-ness are everywhere these days. Doom, gloom, and woe-is-me tales have gained traction across the land. But every now and then, you run into someone who is actually excited about what lies ahead. This person is stoked! (To stoke is to stir up and fuel a fire.)

What's up with this Pollyanna? Doesn't she know how bad things are? Isn't she aware that companies are shedding jobs, people are losing homes, and the prospects for better days are nowhere in sight?

Of course she does. A stoked person is not stupid. She's also not stuck. And because she's not stuck, she is free to create a better future, to seek out other positive souls and to write a stronger and more satisfying chapter than the one we are all enduring right now.

Which begs the question: Is it possible for a stuck person to get stoked? So glad you asked. The answer is Yes!

Here's a formula to try. It's an adaptation of Richard Beckhard's Change Formula that looks like this:

$$C = (D + V + FS) > I$$

and means this: **Change** happens when the combination of **Dissatisfaction** plus **Vision** plus **First Steps** is greater than **Inertia**.

Most people can tell you in great detail what they are Dissatisfied with in their jobs, their relationships, their kids, their lives. Step one is pretty easy.

The next step, articulating a Vision, is a little trickier. Perhaps you can come up with a laundry list—a wish list—of things you would like, but putting them together into a vision is a struggle. Why? We're not taught or encouraged to dream. A vision is a dream of what could be.

Without a vision it is impossible to outline First Steps. But even when you can lay out a vision, sometimes you have no clue what to do first. If you get stuck here, Change is impossible.

Let's say you can describe all three of these elements. The final step is to be sure that they are strong enough together to overcome the Inertia that keeps you stuck.

What is inertia? Unscientifically, it's stuff like your partner's discomfort when you talk about Change. Your lack of time or money. Your belief that you need your boss's permission. The fact that your kids are in school. That you need to lose ten pounds or finish school or wait until the laundry is dry. Inertia is the stuff that is sometimes hard to put your finger on that keeps you firmly stuck in an unhappy place.

That inertia is the noise in your mind. Those tired old stories that don't work for you anymore. The fear that gets stirred up as you listen to the news. That false belief that you need somebody stronger, wiser, richer, or more important to get you out of your bad place.

No, you don't. You need to recognize that you live life in chapters and that this one, although it may be grim, will have an end. More important, you must realize that you have some control over how the end gets written. And what chapter gets written next.

There are two dimensions in working with this equation. One is willingness; the other is ability. Some people simply do not have the ability to work through major life changes. Most people do. Whether or not they—you—have the willingness to do the work, to feel the discomfort, to take the risk of changing your outlook, your associations, your habits, or your ideas is another question altogether. Only you can answer it. When you do in the affirmative, it's amazing what can happen.

Don't stay stuck, get stoked! Use the Change formula to envision and begin writing your next chapter. Your optimism and enthusiasm will encourage others.

Having Your All

You can have it all! Magazine articles tell you so, television shows tell you so, books written by famous people tell you so. The message is always upbeat and lively, encouraging you to go, go, go after every opportunity to get ahead.

To the extent that these messages attempt to motivate positive self-impressions and constructive behavior, there seems little to argue with. Perhaps, however, we need to question the major premise. Is it necessary to "have it all?"

To some, having it all means family, friends, a decent job and a good place to live. While this is admirable, it is, according to current ideas, small potatoes. In the new version of success, family and friends are often taken for granted, a mere backdrop on your life's stage. Having it all today means a glorious and powerful career, a mansion worth millions, ecstasy in your personal relationships, and the winning attitude that keeps you constantly striving for more. Oh yes, and let's add the outward composure that tells the world you handle your life with ease and style because, after all, you're worth it.

It's a seductive picture. You could easily become convinced that if you got up early enough, worked like a (purposeful) demon all day and thought late into the night, you would someday, somehow have it all. But what exactly would you have? Imagine sitting before an enormous banquet table laden with all your favorite foods. Your favorite entertainers are performing and beautiful people hail you at frequent intervals. How much of that food could you ingest before you became ill? Could you truly appreciate the entertainers? Would you remember all the beautiful people and what they said to you?

Having it all demands a lot of time and attention, first to get it and then to protect it. Having it all poses incredible pressures. And it sates all the senses, robbing us of the opportunity to fully enjoy any of it.

You *can* have it all. You might even convince yourself that you can appreciate it all. If so and if you are willing to pay the price, then by all means go for it. But it might be a better idea to have just slightly less than all and revel in it. Pour your heart and energy into the things you select for yourself. Savor them. Delight in them. Labor purposely for them. You'll soon find that you can retire at night pleased with your efforts and proud of your accomplishments no matter what popular culture says you should want.

I Believe in You

I believe in you. These are four of the simplest words in our language, yet how powerful they are. Most of us take pleasure in saying these words to friends or associates who are experiencing a particular difficulty. We like to reassure others, to let them know that even though they may be struggling with extreme adversity, we know they have what it takes to pull through.

When we say, "I believe in you," to someone in trouble, we often imbue that person with renewed strength and determination. We help the individual understand that he or she has the skills and/or fortitude to overcome a difficulty and grow stronger in the process. We offer support, understanding and friendship—valuable gifts in a time of need.

How often do you say, "I believe in you" to yourself? Do you believe in yourself or do you see every difficulty in your life as the natural result of a dumb decision you made?

Are you accident-prone, mistake-prone or failure-prone? Do you often wonder what happened when something goes right? If so, it's time for a change. Treat yourself as you would a friend who is down on his or her luck. Instead of berating yourself with words like fool and idiot, try taking yourself in hand more patiently.

Keep in mind that although you've made a mistake and you may be upset and confused, you can change the situation. You have options. You have access to other information and opportunities. You'll come out of this okay. Spend some time remembering the hard situations you have dealt with in the past. Remind yourself that you have the guts and strength to overcome problems. Go look in the mirror and say out loud, "I believe in you." Once you convince yourself of that, you'll feel your strength and determination begin to grow again.

I'm Busy!

Busy is a popular word. We say it often: I'm busy. The line is busy. That store is a busy place. This is a busy intersection.

At work and at school we sometimes try to look busy even if we aren't. We hesitate to try a new restaurant if it doesn't look very busy. Busy is an exciting thing to be! It keeps us in the mainstream of life and gives us the semblance of importance. Everyone knows that if they need something done they should give it to a busy person.

Did you know that even when you are bored to tears you are still busy? It's true! What do you say when a friend calls you and says, "Gee, I haven't seen you in a long time, how have you been?" You reply, "Oh, I've been keeping myself busy."

Busy can be taking care of business, watching others take care of business, or thinking about taking care of business. Thinking is a busy activity, but it is not sanctioned in our fast-paced, action-oriented society. Who are the great philosophers of our time? I don't know.

In an effort to make ourselves more clearly understood, I propose that we strike the word busy from the English language. Yes, it would mean taking more time to express ourselves and, heaven forbid, we would have to waste precious moments thinking about what we really mean to say. But wouldn't it be much more satisfying to ask someone what they have been doing and get a real answer than to just hear that they have been busy? Ask ten friends what they've been doing and I'll bet they've all been doing the same thing. They have been busy. Does that mean those ten people are exactly alike? Of course not.

Every one of us is busy answering mail and phone calls, talking to business associates and friends, making plans to implement certain programs, cleaning, cooking, taking care of children, etc., etc., depending upon our occupation. But don't we also spend time remembering, worrying, thinking about someone close to us, avoiding people and things we would rather not deal with on any particular day?

It is not the fact that we are busy, but rather the activities we are busy with that define to a large extent who we are. Let's get rid of the word *busy* to describe ourselves. Let's privately pinpoint the things that occupy our time and thoughts. We are likely to find a gold mine of information about ourselves. Self-discovery can lead to self-appreciation and sometimes to self-improvement. Just think, by getting rid of the word busy, we'll be busy learning!

Independent Woman: Role Model or Reprobate?

As we celebrate our nation's anniversary of independence from British rule, it seems a good time to reflect on the status of independence for women. Although we have come a long, long way from being considered chattel, many women still have uneasy questions about how independent a woman should be. Is it good for a woman to be independent? Is it right? Is it feminine?

For some perspective, let's take a quick glance at history. When our country was founded, women were truly considered property of men. Wives were expected to bring pride to their homes by satisfying their husband's needs and desires; by feeding him well, giving him handsome, well-behaved children and serving as paragons of virtue in the community. If a husband strayed or a child misbehaved, a woman was to blame. And she was shamed within her community.

Daughters, if they were fortunate enough to marry, brought gifts of property to their new husbands, compliments of dear old dad. These gifts were called dowries and they had more than a little to do with a woman's attractiveness.

Femininity back then had as much to do with subservience as comeliness. This, ladies, is our cultural DNA.

And it carried an emotional price. Ann Heilman noted in a 1998 paper written at Manchester Metropolitan University that the political battle for women's rights became an individualized struggle for personal freedom.

"Women [are] slowly withering in ideas and interests; lives [are] becoming less and less fruitful and more and more limited every day because they are not allowed to live their own lives but are always compelled to live the lives of other people. They have no chance of self-development, no work or pursuits of their own; their especial talents are left to lie dormant—their best powers are allowed no sphere of action. They must constantly crush back the aspirations of their own natures, and must stifle the cry of their own individuality."

Fortunately, things change.

Today a woman can choose to marry or not, to have children or not, to wear fashions that appeal to her unique taste, to work, to vote, and to befriend whomever she pleases.

And yet, we sometimes wonder if we are doing the right thing. We have been socialized to be relationship builders and the keepers of goodness.

Enter Candace Bushnell, author of the wildly popular "Sex and the City," who draws from her own life as a single, career-driven woman in New York in the 1980s to present another viewpoint of female independence. She reflects on the times:

We as women didn't really know what to do. We didn't have anybody to look back to. All we knew was that we didn't want to live the lives our mothers had.

So they frolicked with abandon. Men were cast as interesting diversions, not central to a life filled with careers, girlfriends, and social escapades.

And so the pendulum swings. From male property to brazen she-devil in a few short centuries.

Sadly, a stereotype emerged of the independent woman as a power - or money-hungry you-know-what who cares little for others or for the damage she does along her independent way. "The Devil Wears Prada" was a recent workplace representation of this woman.

This stereotype is wrong. A more accurate view of an independent woman is one of self-assurance and tolerance, trustworthiness and generosity. The dictionary defines independent as free from the undue influence, control or determination of another.

An independent woman knows her own mind because she has taken time to experience life and reflect on it. She knows her strengths as well as her limitations and she appreciates both. She recognizes the goodness of relationships while maintaining boundaries necessary for her own health. And she honors her time in history by valuing the struggles of the women who came before her to help pave the way to the future.

An independent woman is a joy to her friends and family. She is an asset to her community, a credit to her country, and a gift to the world. Happy Independence Day, ladies!

Invigorate Your Life

*P*assion is a buzzword that has been bandied about the business world for years. It is a good buzzword, because it entails such things as excitement, deep interest, curiosity, enthusiasm and forward movement. There is an energy to the word that is much needed not only in business but in everyday life.

We become passionless because we get trapped in the mundane aspects of life. We work hard throughout our youth to define who we are and to carve out a niche for ourselves in this vast society. We find efficient ways to handle our daily chores, proficient ways to handle our business dealings, and comfortable ways to spend our leisure time. We develop patterns and routines, using the same words to describe our world and the same actions to move around in it. Our niche gradually becomes a rut.

How do we get some passion—some excitement—back into our lives? First, by realizing that no matter how much we know about life, there is an incredible world all around us that we have not seen or learned about. People—you and I—are fascinating. Why do we think as we do? What makes us happy one minute and sad the next? Why do we strive to achieve things? What makes us tick?

Man has tried for centuries to figure himself out and volumes have been written about the human condition. The same is true for science and industry, for law, for medicine. New learning in any of these areas can be exciting, engrossing, energizing.

Another way to invigorate your life is to keep company with passionate people. (No, I'm not talking about romantic encounters.) Find someone who sees the excitement in life, who constantly thinks of possibilities. Befriend that person. His enthusiasm will rub off. You'll find yourself thinking in broader terms, wondering about possibilities, and maybe taking some chances. You will rediscover fun.

Finally, get involved in something bigger than yourself. Work with others to answer a question, change a situation, or gather new information. You'll learn to appreciate the talents of others as you discover the depths of your own.

Passion, in simple terms, is being excited about life and having an intense desire to live it well. It is possible to increase the passion in your life and it is well worth your effort.

It's Halftime!

*R*emember New Year's Eve, six months ago? Do you remember what was foremost on your mind and in your dreams that formed the basis for your New Year's resolutions? Where are those thoughts and dreams today?

Some may be in the dustbin of recent history—great ideas that had little structure or support to see them through. Some may still be lurking in the recesses of your heart and mind, waiting for the right alignment of stars to come true. Some may have changed a bit from what they were then to what you hope they can be now in light of challenging circumstances.

It's June. Halftime. If you're a sports fan, you know that halftime is when the team retreats from the playing field to huddle in the locker room and discuss what happened during the first half. This discussion is both objective and optimistic. What happened in the first half is history; a clear-eyed assessment of how it came to be is important. The second half is still to be played and the outcome is anybody's guess. Here optimism, built on objective understanding, fuels new effort.

Great plays may have been made in the first half; great blunders, too. Helping individuals on the team come to grips with their successes or disappointments creates the opportunity to change their focus, interaction, and results in the second half. Coaches are critical in helping players see both mistakes and opportunities to improve.

Here's the best thing about halftime: It doesn't matter what the other team is thinking! The focus is on improving your team's performance and adjusting to the talent and energy levels of the day.

How did you play the first half of this year? Did you have a clear objective or set of goals when the year started? Were you serious about them or did you wait to see how things would shape up? What has worked to your satisfaction so far? What surprises did you encounter?

June is a happy month in Wisconsin. Summer arrives with its season of barbeques, baseball, beach parties, and a more relaxed way of living thanks to brighter sunshine and longer, warmer days. What a wonderful opportunity to take some time to reflect on the first half of the year and adjust as needed to make yourself a winner in the second half.

Here's a suggestion for your halftime review. Take a look at your calendar over the past six months. Note where you invested your time. Who were you with? What activities did you undertake? What results have you seen so far?

Are there certain people or events that could be added to your social or business mix to help you gain ground? If so, make appointments to include them. Are there others to be limited or eliminated entirely? It can be difficult to reduce time with certain people, especially if you have given it freely in the past. But making these kinds of choices is an important step in building success over time.

Consider carefully whether your allocation of time and attention supports or diminishes your goals. Talk to a trusted colleague, friend, or mentor who can help you see clearly and who may have additional ideas or resources to offer. With first half results and objective input, you may discover that some adjustments are necessary.

Make these adjustments with confidence and a sense of anticipation. The second half of the year is beginning and anything can happen! Set it up to give yourself every chance of winning. Then go play with commitment and enthusiasm. The 'score' will be the score when the year draws to a close. Remember, you win some and you lose some. But the way you played can be a rich source of satisfaction, no matter the outcome.

Job Shopping:
It's All About Mindset

*L*ooking for a new job is never easy and it seems as though the older we get, the more challenging it becomes. Even though fifty is the new thirty in so many ways, looking for a job when you're no longer a fresh-faced debutante can be scary. What makes it so intimidating?

First, there's the overall environment. We live in an intensely competitive, global, 24/7 world. It takes an incredible amount of energy to compete; even more to excel.

Next, there's technology. A dizzying array of digital assistants facilitate connectivity and keep businesses humming around the world. For women who have been out of the workforce or who lack training or experience with emerging technologies, this anxiety can be keen.

And then there are the boss issues. The prospect of working for a younger boss is very difficult for some women, especially if they endured significant conflict in raising children.

But the greatest impediment to job shopping is the nagging self-doubt that simmers inside. Am I good enough? Smart enough? Do I look okay? Can I keep up? Am I too old? These questions can cripple even the most optimistic job seeker. To counteract them and bolster your confidence, try these tips to create a strong and positive mindset.

Play to your strengths. It's easy to get dragged down by the things you can't do (yet), but there's no future in that line of thought. Catalog your abilities and accomplishments and sit down with a friend to practice sharing them. Give special attention to how your skills can specifically serve an employer of interest.

Be willing to learn. A job search can put you face-to-face with fear of the unknown or even a sense of inadequacy. But not knowing something is a temporary state when you're open to learning. Raising your hand to ask a question or availing yourself of training materials and resources marks you as a person worth cultivating.

Take it easy. There is a job out there for you! Avoid the temptation to take a job, any job, just to end the anxiety of job hunting. When you hold out for a position that truly plays to your best talents and career goals, everyone wins.

Maintain your energy. You know the basics of keeping yourself physically fit—proper nutrition, plenty of rest, lots of water, and regular exercise. Emotional fitness is another important aspect of maintaining energy and it requires such things as healthy self-conversations, supportive friends, positive reading materials, and an expectation of success.

Expect a good outcome. The fact of the matter is if you think you can, you'll try. If you think you can't, you'll punt. Pay attention to the stories you tell yourself about your life so far. Has your life been one of learning and adventure or suffering and endurance? You may be surprised at how many women project the latter and how detrimental it is to a job search effort. Expect good things!

Be appreciative of people's time. When you let people know that you genuinely value their time and support, you create alliances that last beyond the immediate job search. Express your appreciation with handwritten notes and personal phone calls.

Finally, remember that while technical and functional skills will always be important to employers, maturity and life experience are strong assets, too. Can you develop a keen understanding of the business issues at hand? Your judgment will be valued. Can you work respectfully with a wide variety of people? Your flexibility and courtesy will be appreciated. Do you bring positive energy to the team? You'll help everyone accomplish more.

Be mindful of all your assets, cultivate a positive mindset, and approach your search with energy and confidence. Your new job awaits!

Let Me Decide!

Doesn't it bug you when people make decisions for you? Ever since childhood when Mom decided you would eat your green beans before getting any ice cream and Dad decided you would spend your allowance on college instead of albums or tapes or junk food, the reasons other people gave for making decisions for you were that they were older or that they knew better what was best for you.

In a lot of instances, this was exactly correct. But now that you are older, more experienced, and have set your own goals, you should be allowed to have the final say in important matters concerning you. Matters such as obtaining loans for cars or houses, getting a better job either within your company or with another one, spending the government's money on things you feel are important, etc.

But what happens instead? A loan officer will say he thinks you would be biting off more than you could chew by adding another monthly payment to your current responsibilities. Upper management doesn't feel you are quite qualified or ready to accept a new position. The government spends money as it sees fit regardless of your outrage because—and here's the classic answer—the experts know a lot more than you do about what needs to be taken care of and how to best go about taking care of it.

Do you have any recourse in situations like these when other people insist on making decisions for you? In some cases, no. But there are times when you are just as responsible for losing your opportunity to decide as are the people who usurp your right. Too often, you don't ask seriously for what you want. Too often you don't say how important something is to you. Too often you don't let others know just what you are willing to do in order to reach your goal. Too often, you simply turn the decision over to someone else.

Perhaps it is time to look calmly, intelligently, and carefully at the many options before you and vow to make your own decisions. The steps are few, but none is easy: Accept responsibility, plan thoughtfully, believe in yourself and then decide for yourself. There's really no one better qualified.

Let's Grow!

*A*re you concerned with your image? Do you protect this image by saying what others expect you to say instead of what you really think? Are you a stuffed shirt? A Harry Hardguy? A Patty Perfect?

Do you ever think about how much of your ability you actually use in an average day? Do you hold yourself back from new things because you are afraid of failure? Do you avoid looking foolish at all costs?

Do you believe in mischief? Can you laugh at the preposterousness of life? Or do you tend to blame people, circumstances and the weather when life becomes particularly difficult?

This column explores questions like these for the purpose of making us think about ourselves and our lives in order to grow in strength, confidence, and self-acceptance. The work is based on three core beliefs:

1. Within each and every one of us there is incredible potential that can and should be tapped.

2. Each of us is directly responsible for the quality of our lives. This means, of course, that we have to be completely

honest with ourselves. It is not the boss or the economy or fate that makes our lives good or bad. It is our own thoughts and actions. Period.

3.   If we truly believe in our potential and seriously direct our thoughts and actions toward positive goals, we will become stronger individuals with happier lives.

Growth and change don't happen overnight. These things take time. And effort. And as human beings, we are natural 'fraidy cats. We don't like to make mistakes or be corrected or take any but the most minimal of risks. We prefer comfort to discomfort. We look for support, encouragement, and cooperation.

Yes, well. The fact is that we all have our share of foibles, quirks, bad habits and inhibitions. But we also have the strength and ability (potential, remember?) to overcome these things.

I invite you to join me to think in positive ways about who you are, and to challenge yourself to grow bigger and better. It sure makes life a lot more fun than counting the number of days without sunshine or rain.

Living is Easy

L iving is easy. It must be. Billions of people do it every day. Hearts beat, brains function, people live. From childhood on, we learn how to care for ourselves and to function in our surroundings. After many years of practice, living becomes an unconscious habit.

You and I know many people who live just like this, setting schedules, programming their systems to carry out their responsibilities—in short, functioning. But active living—living to enjoy life and living with style, however humble—that is something far different.

The active person lives with energy, enthusiasm, and joy. To this person, life is not a thing to be endured—a jail sentence—it is a grand adventure filled with innumerable challenges, treasures, and delights. The person who loves life participates in as many of life's opportunities as he or she can and reacts to life in full measure.

This person is distinctive in appearance, speech and action. The activity within shines through her eyes as excitement, curiosity, often merriment; oftener still, wisdom. Her voice is richer, warmer, and livelier. Her conversation is animated and satisfying to her partner. She listens. She laughs. She interacts sincerely and makes her conversation partner feel good because of the attention she gives so freely. She is interested in everything and everyone.

Such a person is infectious. He makes one want to open up and enjoy life as much as he does. This kind of living is not easy. It requires a self-acceptance and an understanding of life not easy to come by in this age of frantic strivings and private doubts. It means being open to others, even those who might hurt you, for in knowing them, you find more complete knowledge of yourself. It requires consistency, courage, a sense of humor and the tenacity to be who you are and to enjoy the life that you choose despite society's urging to be like everyone else.

If you are such a person, congratulations! Live your life to the fullest with the knowledge that you enrich others by doing so. If you'd like to become such a person, study one you know. Emulate his or her manner, but remember it is *you* you want to become more of, not someone else you want to become more like.

Makin' it in a Man's World

O nce upon a time, there were many jobs that belonged almost exclusively to men. Construction sites, aeronautics labs, the New York Stock Exchange, even some political offices were off-limits to women. But that changed a long time ago. In fact, women infiltrated the most sacrosanct of men's cabals more than 135 years ago when Victoria Claflin Woodhull became the first female U.S. presidential candidate nominated by the National Radical Reformers. That was in 1872!

A year later, Ellen Swallow Richards was the first woman admitted to MIT (Massachusetts Institute of Technology). She went on to become the first female professional chemist in the U.S.

While some people still like to grouse about "a man's world," the truth is that woman have distinguished themselves in many male dominated fields.

Take construction, for instance. The National Association of Women in Construction started out as Women in Construction in Fort Worth, Texas in 1953. Sixteen women started it. By 2003, there were 975,000 women in construction.

How about aerospace? On September 26, 1910, Bessica Raiche completed a solo flight in an aircraft she and her husband built, making her the first woman aviator in the U.S. In 1943, Women Airforce Service Pilots flew 60 million miles on ferry missions during WWII. By then, half a million women (36 percent of the workforce) were working in the aviation industry.

There were early pioneers in the sciences, too. In 1847, Maria Mitchell discovered a comet; she went on to become a professor of astronomy and director of the college observatory at Vassar. In 1849, Elizabeth Blackwell earned her M.D. degree from the Medical Institution of Geneva, New York. She wrote *Pioneer Work in Opening the Medical Profession to Women* in 1895.

Grace Murray Hopper, born in 1906, created computer programs that used mathematical equations computers could interpret. She pioneered COBOL.

The first woman graduated with a chemical engineering degree from MIT in 1923. In 1952, the Society of Women Engineers was formed.

Let's look at business and finance. In 1934, Lettie Pate Whitehead became the first female director of a major corporation at Coca-Cola Company. Muriel "Mickey" Siebert was the first woman to own a seat on the New York Stock Exchange in 1967. Five years later, Juanita Kreps became the first woman director of NYSE.

Katherine Graham became president of the *Washington Post* when her husband died in 1963. But this was long after Mary Katherine Goddard became the first woman publisher (*Providence Gazette*) in

1766 and the first printer to offer copies of the Declaration of Independence in 1777.

Which brings me back to politics. In 1932, Hattie Wyatt Caraway of Arkansas was the first woman elected to the U.S. Senate. The following year, Frances Perkins became the first female member of a presidential cabinet. FDR appointed her Secretary of Labor. In 1964, Margaret Chase Smith of Maine became the first woman nominated for President by a major political party at the Republican National Convention in San Francisco.

Finally, lest we believe that only men take stupid risks, Annie Edson Taylor, a schoolteacher from Michigan, was the first person to go over Niagara Falls in a barrel. That was in 1910. She survived.

Women who break into traditionally male roles confront a number of obstacles. On-the-job discrimination, unequal bathroom access, and a lack of child-care options are common issues. But one of the biggest challenges women face is the negative attitude they encounter away from work. Raised eyebrows and critical remarks, often from friends and family, can hurt even the most independent of souls.

Still, women who have something to accomplish tend to develop a certain social indifference. They don't view the world in terms of who owns it, but rather by the things that can be discovered and invented. It's always been that way.

The pioneers I've noted here may or may not have been rabble-rousers. They may or may not have been mothers. I'm sure they had more than a few difficult days and they probably wondered from time to time whether they were doing the right thing. That's the nature of progress.

If you are that rare woman in a male-dominated environment, remember these women and the amazing things they achieved. With patience, persistence, and a deaf ear toward naysayers, you can do the same. Maybe someday a writer will discover your success and catalog it for a new generation of pioneering women.

Not Pollyanna!

A short while ago, an individual told me that although he didn't agree with many of my thoughts, he considered my column basically good. He felt much of it was pretty Pollyanna-ish, but commented that if more people thought the way I do, the world would be a pretty okay place.

I appreciated his perspective and feedback and considered his Pollyanna remark. In my mind, Pollyanna thinking is equivalent to viewing the world through rose-colored glasses; to shutting out those aspects of life that are harsh, cruel or unpleasant; pretending that all is well despite real difficulty. This is not the same as adopting a positive outlook toward life. What's the difference?

A positive outlook acknowledges the difficulties of life, but refuses to be incapacitated by them. It is based on a belief that one can have an impact on a situation, and that a positive outcome is possible. In fact a positive attitude draws strength from this positive expectation. Positive thinkers expect good things to happen and they do whatever they can to ensure such good results.

In no way is true positive thinking wishful, fantastic, or inert. It involves dreaming, sure. We all dream of good things to come. But positive people take action to make their dreams come true. They are not strangers to disappointment and hardship. They simply refuse to let setbacks take away their vigor, hope and striving for better things.

The difference between positive and Pollyanna thinking is sort of like the difference between courage and bravery. Courage recognizes danger and acts in the face of it. Bravery is not necessarily cognizant of true danger, so charges forth fearlessly. It may look like courage, but lacks the intentional resolve.

The second point that seems worth making is that if everyone thought the way I do, how boring life would be, and how unfortunate. It is only through the interchange of ideas and interaction with people who are different from ourselves that we learn and grow. I am reminded of a quote I read once upon a time that said, "It is good to rub and polish our minds against those of others." Precisely! If we were not constantly trying out new thoughts and receiving feedback and correction, we would soon become stale as month-old cookies. There would be no flavor, no texture, and no zest left to intrigue or satisfy us.

I heartily encourage a positive attitude because if you start out thinking, "I can't," you won't. But I also encourage debate and discussion because different opinions and ideas are vital to continued development.

Not Your Style? Why Not?

How many times have you decided not to try something because you were afraid of what your friends would think? Be it a new hobby, a new occupation, a new hairstyle or a new way of thinking, most of us hold back if we think it might upset those who know us. We don't want to act out of character. We don't want to disturb the image others have of us.

We all know what potential is. Most of us think we have plenty of it, even though it may be hidden. But many of us refuse to test our potential. Because we are unsure of what others will think, we hesitate to reach beyond normal limits, to try something a little different from our regular activities.

What a pity that is. What a shame to limit ourselves to the types of things that others expect of us. Who knows what kind of satisfaction we might find in some unexplored area? Who knows what kind of success? How can we be so sure that some other endeavor won't work simply because on the surface it doesn't appear to be our kind of thing?

Each one of us has our own life to live, our own song to sing. Why not live it joyfully, openly, and with an enthusiasm to try new things? Why be restricted by those who would say, "That's not your style."

Why not bring our skeptics along, showing them ever so carefully and gently that there is a tremendous wonderland outside their own worlds just waiting to be explored and enjoyed. The more people we can get singing, the richer our harmony will be. Even off-key voices are welcome!

Online Presence: Is it You?

*T*he age of technology has given us all amazing new ways to be more visible and tell our stories far and wide. In a competitive world with lots of noise, sometimes stories get embellished. Truth is, embellishment has become part of the process; it's even expected online. After all, who in their right mind wants to be an average person living a routine life earning mere bill-paying wages?

This tendency to exaggerate presents a real challenge to employers, employees, and anyone seeking help or a date online.

Let's start with the workplace. Depending on the expert, estimates range from forty percent to over fifty percent of people who lie on their resume. Some of these are so-called white lies, like inflating the number of people they managed. Some overstate academic achievements. Some claim job titles they never held.

Having the ability to post resumes online seems to strengthen the temptation to exaggerate. With a few mouse clicks, it's easy to highlight one particular set of skills for this job, while calling on a different set of credentials or omitting certain details for that job. Pretty soon it seems natural enough to bend a fact here, cut a corner there, and start believing that close enough is good enough. It's not.

Sooner or later the lies get exposed. Worse, the person who gets a job based on a lie lives in fear. What a way to diminish productivity.

Then there's the wholesale fiction that passes for personal profiles on dating sites. I always laugh when my friends tell me about the person who showed up suddenly looking fifteen years older than her stated age or looking nothing like the Adonis he described. Where's the sense in that kind of exaggeration?

Chat rooms are filled with people who write amazing and sometimes horrifying things from the privacy of their anonymous perch behind a computer screen. The combination of privacy and anonymity brings out a very human tendency to say things you wouldn't normally say. If you ever told tall tales in the dark as a kid, you know what this feels like. If you have teenagers, you've probably seen them try on a whole bunch of different personalities. While this is normal, technology enables fantasy in sometimes-tragic ways.

When you appear online, is it you or is it a figment of your best imagination? Beware your answer because with every electronic snapshot you post, you are creating your reputation.

Here are a couple of tips to keep it real and make it good.

- Tell the truth. By all means, highlight your accomplishments, but if you were the only accountant in a small company, don't put yourself out there as "Chief Financial Officer." When you post a photo, make it reasonably current.

- Make sure your spelling, grammar, and punctuation portray you as the intelligent, thoughtful person you are. Spell check is a good starting point, but don't rely on it exclusively. Irregularities in word choice or punctuation can damage your credibility in short order.

- ♦ Limit hip, slang language, especially when it runs counter to your personality or belies your age. It's embarrassing when people from different generations try to fit an age and lifestyle that is not real.

- ♦ When using email as a primary means of communication, be thoughtful about the words you choose and the style you use. Conveying warmth without being overly familiar is difficult. So is being direct without appearing dismissive or rude.

It's true that technology allows us greater visibility and helps us do many things a lot faster than we used to. But beware the traps of speed and star-polishing. Before you post anything, ask yourself: Is it true? Is it me? Is it helping to build the kind of reputation I truly want and deserve?

Ready to Hang it Up? Think Again.

There seems to come a time in the lives of most people to mentally lean back, put the feet up, flip on the tube and cease striving. I say mentally because the picture I have described does not necessarily include the physical activity, but is more permanent than mere relaxation. It depicts a sort of mental resignation.

This mental resignation occurs when an individual either feels pretty well set or decides within himself that no amount of effort on his part will result in any significant change or advance in his life. Regardless of whether this kind of slacking off occurs at an early age or late in life, it is tragic.

Claude M. Bristol writes in *The Magic of Believing*: "Your life is your thinking and the result of your thinking processes." By thinking that there is nothing new, exciting or profitable still in store for you, you create a future that is stagnant, unexciting and certainly unfulfilling. Why would anyone choose this?

Does anyone really believe that he or she has heard, seen, read, and experienced it all? I can't believe that. It is simply not possible. Do we run out of energy? No. New knowledge and new experience is fantastically energizing. Do we wear out physically? Sure, but generally mental resignation triggers physical degeneration. We've all seen our share of elderly people in great shape. All of them are vitally interested in life.

So why do people both young and old throw in the towel and coast through life? I believe there are two major reasons. One is that they hear people tell them so often that they will never get what they want, never accomplish what they strive for, and never realize their impossible dreams. Eventually they succumb to this mental browbeating and abandon their hopes and dreams because what they hear over and over is what they ultimately believe.

The second reason is that they never had a burning desire to accomplish their goal in the first place. Because of this, they lost patience and gave up too soon. And because they did not really expect success, they may have been disappointed but were not surprised when they did not achieve it.

Friends, if you feel inclined to hang it up, ask yourself why. Have you set your immediate sights too high? Notice I said immediate. I firmly believe that if you think a thing, you can achieve it. But it takes time. Give yourself time. Achieve your goals in increments.

Ignore the naysayers. These are the people who never had the courage to become what they were capable of becoming and who loudly scorn the audacity of enthusiastic others. Encourage others in their endeavors; help where you can. Stay involved; look for challenges. Remember that whatever you believe you can do, in time you will do. What results can you expect? A longer life, perhaps. A happier life, without doubt.

Reclaim Your Independence!

After a long, chilly spring season, summer now simmers in Wisconsin. Remarkably, it is already time for another Fourth of July celebration! Only this year, a lot of women are feeling anything but independent. Hemmed in by financial worries, family challenges, or relationship issues and driven by the pace of life in general and the incessant call of our technologies, how is anyone supposed to feel like celebrating? Independence, what's that?

I will confess: I am in technological rehab, reclaiming my independence from the Internet. What started out as an innocent daily ritual of checking horoscope, weather, and headlines—in that order—grew over time to a morning routine that chewed up several hours. Worse, it filled my mind with bad news, nasty comments, and general anxiety over things over which I have no control. What a way to start a day!

As a writer, I justified my time online as research and observation of my fellow humans. I reasoned that the more news I had and the more insight I could gain from reading comments following online stories, the broader my understanding of life outside my community and thus the more valid my commentary. I'm pretty good at rationalizing.

What I could not explain away were the hours that flew by with little to show for my time. Deadlines became more difficult to meet. Writing started to get harder because my mind wanted to jump around like fans at a Badger football game. I had a hard time focusing and maintaining concentration. For a while, I rationalized this, too. Menopause.

But rationalization didn't change my growing unease or dissatisfaction. One day I read a book review in the Wall Street Journal that pointed to some new research about the impact technology is having on our brains. Because this question has been on my mind in recent years, I bought the book. In it, the author described my very behavior. He had fallen prey, too.

What does this have to do with independence? Everything. The notion of making choices may be more important today than ever before simply because we have more choices to make. How often do you check email? How quickly do you respond to text messages? How much time do you spend reading or commenting to news online?

These appear to be simple, maybe simplistic, questions, but they drive at the heart of independence. When you are drawn into repetitive behaviors that begin to encompass more of your life than you like, you begin losing your freedom. Does that sound extreme? Perhaps it is, but I challenge you to walk away from all your technologies for a day. Just one day. No email. No texting. No computer access. No telephone. No TV. No video. Most people would go crazy.

Those who succeed, however, may discover a lost world of nature. Or their families. Or themselves. What wonderful subjects to study! What wonderful freedom to reclaim.

An ironic coincidence occurred as I was writing this column. I had an email from the husband of my former literary agent notifying his contacts that he was leaving LinkedIn and the rest of social media. Given his prominence in literary circles, I called to ask why. "I wanted my life back. I wanted to hear myself think."

He admitted it was a drastic step and potentially an unwise one. Only time will tell, but he relishes the notion of reclaiming his time to invest as he sees fit. He feels happy, lighter, even powerful. "It's my personal declaration of independence." No kidding, he really said that.

As you consider the quality of your time this Independence Day, take the radical step of reclaiming some that has been co-opted by technology. Put your smart phone down during dinner. Stop checking email right before bedtime. Resist the urge to text your friends about the fantastic fish tacos you had for lunch. When you can separate yourself from the frenzy, even for a brief moment now and then, you will begin to re-experience the joy of independence. You might also begin to remember what confidence, happiness, and power feel like.

The "Overnight" Success

We are fooled sometimes into thinking that things happen overnight. Let's say, for instance, that you meet someone you have not seen in two weeks and this person is ten pounds lighter. You may think you last saw your friend only yesterday or several days ago at most. The illusion is that this friend lost ten pounds overnight, quickly and painlessly.

The illusion, of course, is false. While you were busy in the two-week interval, you did not see the daily effort that went into your friend's "overnight" weight loss.

You might also know of someone who has attained a goal set one year ago. Looking back, the year has passed quickly and once again the illusion of sudden success appears. But throughout that year, the effort was consistent, targeted and expended daily.

What is time but a succession of days? What is success but the outcome of repeated effort? When you set a goal and look out into the future, the way may seem long, the task impossible. Yet you know that when you reach the future and look back, time will have flown.

We make powerful choices each day of our lives. Do you use your days purposefully or do you cast them aside for better, more promising tomorrows? Aristotle observed, "We are what we repeatedly do."

A little bit of effort made each day toward some future dream will gradually bring the dream closer until one day it becomes reality. Others may think it happened suddenly but you will know it took many hours of long, determined effort. The next time you read of the overnight success, don't believe it for a moment. Remember that any success is the culmination of consistent, purposeful work.

Start now on your overnight success. Remind yourself each day of the goal you have set and spend some time pursuing it. In the end, your friends will be amazed at how easily you succeeded.

The Power of Commitment

*H*ave you ever wondered why, when there are so many things you would like to do, so few of them ever get done? There are many reasons—each of us has our own list—but they could all be summed up in one word: commitment. Unless and until we make a commitment to accomplish our goals, we will not achieve them.

Let's say, for example, that you want to lose ten pounds. Your reasons might be to look younger, feel better, have your clothes fit better, feel more confident, lower your blood pressure, or be able to work longer without becoming fatigued. The list could go on and on. All of these reasons make you feel that it would be nice to lose ten pounds.

Have you made a commitment? No. You've simply listed reasons why you'd like to lose weight. Will you change your behavior? Based on this wishful thinking, no. You will not lose weight or even make a serious effort to do so until you truly make up your mind to change your behavior.

We make commitments when something becomes important to us in terms of health, safety, occupation or self-esteem. How? By deciding deep down within ourselves that it is time to change. Not because someone else thinks we should, but because we want to. When we make a commitment to something, we set a process in motion that helps us achieve our goals.

A commitment is made up of several parts. First, it entails a belief that the goal is reachable and that you have the skills or abilities necessary to achieve it. Second, you must set a deadline for accomplishing your goal. Without setting a deadline, you are simply engaging in more wishful thinking. Third, with a deadline set, you must regularly monitor your progress. By repeating the goal over and over to yourself, you keep your actions on track and moving closer toward the goal. Also by keeping a continuous eye on your progress, you can easily spot and correct minor deviations.

The final phase of commitment is attaining the goal. Realizing success. You know that success breeds success. Commitment to one goal can lead to commitment to others. It makes sense. If something is worth doing—if it's worth your time—it deserves the kind of commitment needed to get it done well.

Start small. Start slowly. But today, right now, pick one thing and make a commitment to achieve it. Write down your goal. Set a deadline. Get started. You'll be amazed over time at how many of those things you'd like to get done actually get done.

What Do You Want to Be When You Grow Up?

hat do you want to be when you grow up? This seemingly innocuous question makes two subtle but important assumptions. One is that sometime during the course of your life you must be something and the other is that one day you will grow up.

The first of these assumptions again seems fairly innocent. It is common to ask children what they want to be and the question, of course, is one of occupation. This question typically prompts big dreams. Possibilities seem endless to children and the majority of fields are wide open.

Today, unemployment has crimped the availability of certain choices and cramped the ability to dream. Job selection by those free to choose is often based on money. Where is the largest salary? Natural abilities are bent to conform to the skills required by the big-money jobs. Too often the result is dissatisfaction and unhappiness with the choice.

Some role selections have fallen out of favor with the general public. Motherhood and housewifery are two examples. Others, thanks to the media, are glamorized as never before. Construction workers are modern day heroes. Women are no longer portrayed as secretaries; today they are CEOs. Truck drivers had a few glory years during the CB craze, and Sally Ride gave women a shot at space. What do you want to be has become a harder question to answer, but the pressure is on to answer it, and answer it well.

The best starting place is still your own personal interests. What do you like to do? Have you a particular passion? Give serious thought to your present occupation. If people annoy you, is it wise to work in public relations? If numbers frighten you, why work as a cashier? It is true that many people stay in unsatisfying jobs because alternative choices are scarce. If this describes you, then perhaps a hobby or leisure time activity could best satisfy your interests.

The second assumption is that we must grow up. The problem here is one of definition. Shall we define growing up in terms of years, experiences, maturity of perception or sophistication? What is the magic number of years, and how do we measure the other qualities?

The pressure to grow up and be something is greater today than ever before. Preppies, yuppies and a host of other unnamed super achievers are the result. They remind me of greyhounds: lean, strong and ever eager to compete. But they often seem breathless and high-strung as well.

What do you want to be when you grow up? Might it make sense, regardless of occupation, to want to be productive, happy, satisfied with your accomplishments and reasonably aware of other people? Might we define success in terms of personal contentment rather than in terms of money, power or prestige? The definitive answer will not likely come until we draw our final breaths, but I, for one am banking on the former.

Women of Achievement

September is national Women of Achievement month and I have a question for you: Are you on the list?

Typical honorees include famous and visible women like Oprah Winfrey and Hillary Rodham Clinton. But lesser known women are highlighted, too. Mary Cassatt, for example, was the first American Impressionist artist. In a twist of irony, she gained fame for her depictions of women doing ordinary tasks, especially with children, even though she was never married and had no children of her own.

Mary McLeod Bethune, an educator, was a pioneer in providing educational opportunities for African Americans. A statue of her stands in Washington, D.C., the first depicting any woman or African American in any park in the nation's capital. Among her many contributions, Mary founded the National Council of Negro Women in 1935.

Madame Marie Curie fought Russian oppression in Poland to pursue her education as a child and young adult. She is legendary for her discovery of radium, and for being the first woman to win a Nobel Prize for Physics and the first person to win a second Nobel Prize. It was for Chemistry.

Each of these women has made an impression on the world. As I reflected on their achievements, I wondered about the nature of success today and the ways in which it is recognized. I thought, too, of how other-driven most women are, thanks to a host of influences.

I believe we live in a world filled with too many distractions and false notions of success and achievement. Women are encouraged to compete for bigger jobs and heftier paychecks to support lifestyles of glamour and celebrity. And to do it all while looking like a supermodel.

Standing in stark contrast to famous women is my grandmother. An obscure woman who died in her early sixties, she was not pretty or social and she had no particular claim to fame. However, she changed my life in ways I did not fully appreciate until long after she was gone.

Grandma taught me the healing power of deep listening and the freedom and joy of learning to think for myself. Her kitchen was her laboratory and her work was done unbeknownst to any news organization or recognition body. Her humble spirit informs the best of my work today and I will always be grateful for the lessons in patience and respect I learned from her.

You may be one of millions of Wisconsin women who are more like my grandmother than Oprah. Thank heaven for you! Your work is critical.

Maybe you aspire to become famous and perhaps one day your work will be heralded publicly. If so, the elements of success will likely include a singularity of purpose, persistence of effort, and a fundamental belief in yourself and your mission. By all means, follow your calling and your dream.

I have a plaque hanging in my home that reminds me of the true power and sweetness of a woman's success. Here is what it says.

That Woman Is A Success

*Who has an appreciation of the world around her
and her unique place in it...
Who has the capacity to give of herself
and to accept graciously the gifts of others...
Who has a commitment to both her work
and the time she sets aside for play...
Who has the enthusiasm to welcome each new day
with warmth and joy and love.*

Whether your ultimate success is in raising a child, writing a new software program, discovering the next scientific breakthrough, winning athletic competitions, or making fantastic meals, your achievements are gifts to this world. They deserve to be celebrated.

And whether or not your name ever appears in the annals of history, it is already engraved on the hearts of your family and friends. That, my friends, is a lifetime achievement.

You Are What You Think About? Not Quite.

A popular expression today says, "You are what you think about." Well, yes, but... It's not quite that simple. In fact, it is entirely too easy when reading that sentence to be seduced into believing that if only you think a certain way it will be so.

Take success and self-help books, for instance. We read them feverishly because we know that the precepts are sound, the presentation highly inspirational. But what is the end result? This, of course, is up to the individual.

Imaging, the act of seeing oneself in a new successful situation, is a favorite ploy of success purveyors. And yes, it is a powerful tool in creating a new self-image. Fine. Go sit in your recliner every night and for ten minutes imagine yourself the CEO of your favorite corporation, the sleekest person in your social circle, or the most popular parent in your neighborhood. Never mind the fact that you cut corners in your present job, mass consume salty snacks, or have a distinct dislike of children. Just meditate on the ideal you and eventually it will come to pass.

Sorry, folks, it won't work.

Yes, our thoughts determine our actions and it is true that the more positive our thoughts the more likely we are to succeed. But thought is only half of the equation. By itself it is ineffective. Action is the other factor, and it is essential. Go ahead and imagine yourself a certain successful way. Now ask yourself: What is different about me? How am I acting? What am I thinking? What will it take to make the changes necessary to become that new successful me?

Then, get going on the answers. Define the difference. Make plans to change. Act. By all means, think positive thoughts. They will help you to conjure up the better image. But then get out of the ethereal realm and into the real "guts and glory" world. In order to succeed you must do.

It can be incredibly debilitating to read and learn all there is to know about success and then... do nothing with the knowledge. When we have all the answers—the right thoughts—and fail to apply them, well, haven't we failed twice?

Please don't become a victim of vicissitude. Positive thought and determined, energetic action will yield fantastic results. Neglect not the action phase, however, or your sweet dreams will remain just that.

You Go First

*H*ave you ever noticed in this age of me first and YouTube (which is really "MeTube"), how reluctant people are to leave their comfort zones in order to experience something new or solve a problem? I chuckle when I see people's faces say "you go first," even though they don't always say the words.

Once upon a time, I was on vacation with my two daughters in Mexico. We were on an open-air bus tour, learning about the Mayan culture, when we stopped at a remarkable underground lake. A generous ledge allowed us to walk around the perimeter and there was a small area for swimming. The sun poured through an opening high above the ground and shimmered off a long trailing vine, which reached almost to the water's surface. It was a spectacular sight.

On one side, a metal staircase rose 30 feet into the air with platforms at the midpoint and at the top. People were climbing the stairs and jumping off the platforms into the water. Most bobbed to the surface with amazed looks on their faces; some whooped in joy at the experience.

I couldn't resist. Up I went, higher and higher to the top platform, wondering secretly if this was a wise thing to do? My daughters looked on in terror. What would become of them if Mom perished in this foolish act?

The jump from the platform into the cool water was exhilarating and I did it several more times. Eventually, the girls decided to try it from the lower platform. By the time we left, we were feeling excited and proud of our boldness.

Granted, this is an extreme example, but it demonstrates a natural hesitancy that characterizes so much of life today. When change is proposed, you can almost see people shrink a little. If there were dialog bubbles over their heads, they might read: "You go first and if you don't get killed I might follow." And so we get stuck in ways that are not satisfying and sometimes not at all productive, but they feel safe.

It's the frog in the pot story. Put a frog in a lukewarm pot of water and increase the heat ever so slightly over a period of time. Pretty soon the frog is boiling. Having adjusted to the increase in temperature little by little, he never sensed danger. Had you plopped him into a pot of boiling water, he would have jumped to save his life!

Many relationships are like this at home, at work, at school and in the community. Things are not what we would like them to be, but nobody has had the courage to go first in identifying the problem and then attempting a new way to be together. So we wait. We adjust to bad behavior and hope that someday someone will step up.

Going first can be scary, for sure. But when something is not working, you have a responsibility to ask why not. You also have a responsibility to consider what might work better and be willing to suggest a solution. Finally, if you can be bold enough to be the first to try a new act, you grant permission for others to be brave, too.

This last point is important. I was working with an executive in Hungary who wanted to replace a team member who was not perform-ing well. Identifying the lack of performance was the first uncomfort-able issue. But if she was aware of the problem, surely other team members were, too. Indeed, they were waiting for someone to bring it up. The next challenge was to lay out a plan to improve performance or replace the offender. By having the courage to do so, this executive showed the rest of the team how to professionally identify a problem and propose solutions. She went first.

Such is the way of leadership. The unknown is always a little scary. But when you enter it with eyes wide open looking for new possibilities, you may discover unbelievable riches. Imagine the fun of sharing those riches with others. Go ahead. Go first.

Making Adjustments

We plan. We organize. We practice discipline. And we expect these efforts to reward our aspirations or, at the very least, keep us out of trouble.

And then life happens. Curve balls, roller coasters, and our worst nightmares play out. How we adapt matters.

Dolly Parton, internationally famous as a country singer, songwriter, actress, and philanthropist, who happens to be married to the same man she wed in 1966, has this to say:

You cannot direct the wind, but you can adjust the sails.

A Return to Routine

The summer days of more casual living are waning as kids go back to school and business schedules begin to fill again. As vacations, golf outings, and picnics become the memories of summer, our thoughts and energies turn to what the rest of the year will hold.

For many workers in our state, the sad reality is that the routines of jobs and careers have been severed by layoffs or company relocations or closings. Some have established new routines while others struggle to adjust. Families across the nation are adapting to financial constraints by renegotiating priorities and routines.

It makes sense to examine the importance of routine, especially during times of upset or unanticipated change. Family therapists emphasize structure and predictability as critical elements in helping children feel safe and secure. Knowing that certain activities take place on a regular schedule—meals and bedtimes are the most basic—gives children a sense of orderliness that allows them to develop trust and self-confidence.

Adults, too, need some level of structure and routine to feel productive, although the degrees of both structure and routine vary widely. Some people thrive on living in the moment day to day, addressing what presents itself and enjoying the wacky journey of life, while others need to have each day laid out with checklists and timelines to feel okay.

What level of routine is right for you? After the longer, lazier days of summer, what makes you feel energized and newly productive about returning to routine? What hopes spring from this return to greater structure? New goals inspire renewed effort. They also provide a platform for encouraging one another in looking for more rewarding days ahead.

As you transition to new seasons, reflect a moment on seasons past. You will find progress, growth, and maybe an amazing accomplishment or two. Take the lessons to structure your work and build what's next.

Adjusting to Stormy Times

What do you do when you are driving your car and suddenly find yourself in the middle of a raging snowstorm or blinding rain?

Generally, you slow down and proceed with increased caution and attentiveness. If the storm is severe enough, you may pull off the road and wait until the worst of it passes before continuing on. You realize that your health and safety are more important than reaching your destination at a certain time. If someone is waiting for you, you may call or text the situation and let them know you may be late.

What do you do when you encounter a stormy period in your life? If you're like most folks, you don't slow down. You speed up. You may even shift into overdrive, ruminating, fretting, bouncing from one task to another, chasing wildly after anything that resembles a solution to your problem. You lose sleep. Oftentimes, you end up spinning your wheels.

Why is it that we can be so logical when driving in severe weather and so irrational in steering through personal turbulence? Why do we think that by speeding everything up we can find quick and easy relief?

There are times, no doubt, when swift action is not only appropriate, but also necessary. But we must be able to judge a situation and determine correctly when such a time arises. In order to judge effectively and well, we need experience. And experience takes time. We need time to observe, study, test and evaluate before we can make sound judgments. Perhaps we hurry to learn more quickly. More likely, we hurry to get tough times behind us with no thought toward learning.

The next time you encounter a storm on the highway of life, give yourself a break. Take time to slow down. Become a bit more attentive, even cautious if necessary. Adjust to the conditions. You may want to pull over and let the storm pass. Your health and happiness are well worth the delay. Keep in mind, too, that as with all storms and all of life's troubles, this too shall pass.

Are you Proactive or Reactive?

A s you go about your activities at work, school and home, are you proactive or reactive? Do you take the initiative to make things happen or do you scramble to adjust to the changes that happen around you?

You are proactive if you call a family conference when you feel tension building at home. You are reactive if you wait until your child is suspended from school to call his counselor. You are proactive if you schedule idea-sharing meetings with your co-workers. You are reactive when you try to figure out what went wrong after the fact.

Proaction requires attentiveness, thought, and ability. Attentiveness first, because you need to see what is going on around you. If you don't know what's happening, you can't understand context or find a way to connect the dots. What you don't see can hurt you!

Next, you need to think about what you see and formulate ideas for changing a situation or maintaining its best aspects. Thought is essential to being proactive, but thinking is a maligned skill these days. We tend to favor action in any situation, but "Look before you leap" is still good advice.

Finally, to be proactive, you need ability—the ability to get off dead center and put your ideas to work. Great thinking can become heavy thinking if our bottoms remain planted. Think first, of course, but then act. The proactive person pays attention to what is going on, thinks abut the implications and acts accordingly.

What does the reactive person do? The reactive person, by definition, acts in response to something. He is not a forward-looking individual. She probably does not think too deeply about the events of the day, and generally does not make long-range plans for the future.

The reactive person tends to be nervous. He may be especially fearful of the future, for he knows not what to expect. The reactive person likes to blame people, places, and things for her unpreparedness. She will shrug her shoulders at life and ask what more she could have done.

You may detect a proactive bias in this writing and yes, I will admit to it. There are positive aspects of reactionism, however. For one thing, you'll never be accused of counting your chickens before they're hatched. As in all things, there is good and bad, positive and negative in both proaction and reaction.

Are you proactive or reactive? Has your style served you well? If so, be happy. If not, perhaps it is time to reconsider. You can get a jump on tomorrow, today. Or you can spend tomorrow wondering about what happened today.

Beating SAD

Wintertime for a majority of Midwesterners is a time of dreariness and depression, aimlessness and ambivalence. Most of us at some time during the winter feel irritable, out of shape, listless, restless, bored, boxed in and sometimes frantic. We feel cranky without a cause. We don't like the way things are but we have no ambition or energy to change them.

Throughout the winter our tendency is to sit and let things happen instead of making them happen. Our involvement drops with the temperature. Then, with all the suddenness and ferocity of a January blizzard, cabin fever strikes. Restlessness, anxiety, and frustration bat us around inside our homes, schools and offices. If only there was something to do. Or rather, if only there was something we felt like doing!

What ails us is real. It has a scientific name—Seasonal Affective Disorder (SAD)—with a list of symptoms that are right on target: depression, fatigue, sleepiness, weight gain and a craving for carbohydrates. Researchers of the disorder say it is caused by the effect of low winter light levels on the hypothalamus. In other words, we don't get enough sunlight. To alleviate the problem, scientists recommend getting outside in full natural light at least a half hour a day. Even cloudy days provide more and better light than we get inside. Light therapy, psychotherapy and medication are available, too.

What relief we find in these facts. We can feel better knowing that our grumpiness is not entirely our fault. We can feel better, too, knowing that we have some control over the problem. But knowing the solutions, we now face a choice: To get outside a half hour a day, buy a special light, see a shrink, take meds or to stay inside, ignore, and aggravate the problem. Keep in mind that it's not only your health, but your relationships with others that need to be considered as well.

The least expensive solution is also the quickest to start. Go on. Grab your snowshoes, skates, or skis, your sled or toboggan, even your snow blower or shovel and get out into that beautiful winter light. Deny the urge to crawl under the afghan and be hypnotized by the screen. Forget about baking those cookies to keep the kitchen warm unless you don't mind a few extra pounds keeping you warm, too. Try to get up a little earlier than usual to get a jump on your projects for the day. By the end of winter, you can be feeling vigorous and alive instead of ending up another SAD case.

Incidentally, life can sometimes feel like one long, cold winter. The solutions apply. Get moving in order to get past SAD.

From Crabby to Committed

S elf-improvement is an idea that has caught on in a big way. All around the world, people are eating better, shaping up, and becoming more assertive, more loving and happier.

So why, on an individual basis, is it so hard to get started? And why is it that the more a person thinks about self-improvement, the lower that person's self-esteem falls?

The answer, of course, is attitude. You can look at a self-improvement program in terms of all the things that are wrong with you and how important it is that you change these things. Or you can view self-improvement as an exciting new way to live, regardless of where you're starting. Concentration is placed on results of the program—a healthier, more patient, thinner, more active you—rather than on the defects that need correcting.

Think of all the mornings you wake up feeling tired and disgruntled. You don't like the way things are, you wish they were different, but you don't have the energy to change them. It is impossible in this frame of mind to think of anything that would make any difference at all.

Imagine, instead, waking up happy and excited about a new day in which to practice the good qualities of the new person you are aiming to become. This sounds deceptively simple, but it requires a completely different way of thinking—hopeful instead of doubtful, willing to try rather than dully resigned. What a difference. A person in this frame of mind gets a real kick out of self-improvement effort.

Isn't this true in all areas of our lives? We can look at the difficult things and wonder how we will ever overcome them, or we can focus on the terrific results we expect and work steadily toward them.

Are you feeling the need for serious self-improvement? Try these simple steps. 1) Identify what you want to change, briefly and without accompanying self-abuse. 2) Outline specific daily actions—baby steps—you will take to bring about the change. 3) Think about the good results you are working toward before you go to sleep at night. 4) Wake up energized by your new program—happy, excited and eager to continue. With a joyful, expectant attitude, you can't help but succeed. You have already improved your outlook!

Get Out of Your Comfort Zone!

We all know what a comfort zone is and most of us have engineered a very cozy one over the course of our lives. The comfort zone consists of familiar routines, people, ideas, habits, foods, movies, you name it. It is a safe place, a place in which to relax because you know what to expect.

Construction of the comfort zone starts early. As children, we gradually figure out what we like and what we don't. If you are exposed to a wide variety of people, places and things, you may create a comfort zone that is quite large. Of course the opposite is true as well. Stay home on the porch and your comfort zone will be very different from that of the kid who sails off on a bike every morning.

When you live in your comfort zone, you tend to hang around people who think like you do, behave in similar ways, laugh at the same jokes, and generally see the world the way you do. They eat similar food, shop at the same stores, watch the same TV shows and know the local gossip. They also agree that the people you think are weird— are weird.

Just outside the comfort zone is the learning zone, which is by definition uncomfortable. The learning zone if chock full of new ideas, people, strategies, languages, geographies, skills and tools of all sorts. It can look and feel intimidating sometimes, which of course makes sense. It's outside your comfort zone.

It is entirely normal to seek encouragement and guidance to enter the learning zone. Sometimes, however, you need to be pushed into it for your own good. Therapists, enlightened bosses, and professional development experts play this role.

Lurking right outside the learning zone is the panic zone. This is the place where your faculties shut down and you become either hysterical or paralyzed. The panic zone makes you deaf, dumb, and blind. It is not a good place. People who are trained to push you into the learning zone are cognizant of the dangers of shoving too hard.

Looking at this simple model makes it easy to see why most people do not leave the comfort zone with enthusiasm. Our natural inclination is to resist things that make us feel uncertain. We fear landing in the panic zone!

But there is danger in staying too long in the comfort zone. It becomes a rut. People get stuck. They get crabby. Then they get depressed. Thinking hardens into absolutes, which can develop into closely held extremes.

When this happens, the unfamiliar becomes vaguely dangerous and people who are different become scary somehow. Paranoia sets in and the comfort zone becomes a fortress. Hunkering down into your comfort zone is a declaration that you refuse to learn.

Sadly, we all know people like this. They say things like, "That's not how we do it here." "I tried that; it didn't work." "I don't wear that color." "We don't hang out with those people." No opportunity for growth or change here!

But looking at unfamiliarity as an opportunity to learn can be a delightful way of expanding your comfort zone. Feeling the discomfort of a new situation can lead us to think, "I'm outside my comfort zone. I'll slow down and pay attention. Wonder what is here for me to learn?"

The more time you intentionally spend in the learning zone, the larger your comfort zone gets. As your comfort zone expands, it pushes the learning zone out further. In time, the panic zone goes away. Not because you never again encounter something that frightens or rattles you, but because you have trained yourself to manage discomfort and learn. This yields great power! And peace.

Do yourself a favor this spring. Make like a butterfly and burst out of your cocoon! Get out of your comfort zone. Introduce yourself to someone new. Entertain a different point of view. Start a hobby or discussion group and invite strangers. Visit places that are new. Challenge yourself to grow. You'll enjoy your expanding comfort zone and the new possibilities it brings.

Git 'Er Done!

So much to do; so little done. This is the litany of the procrastinator, the dreamer, and the defeated. Does it sound like you?

Are you a procrastinator? Do you put off until tomorrow what you don't feel like doing today? You need to learn self-discipline and how to delay gratification.

Are you a dreamer? Do you forget to take care of the realities of today while you yearn for the promises of tomorrow? You need to set priorities that are grounded in the reality of here and now.

Are you defeated? Have you bought the notion that because you have not succeeded in the past you will not succeed in the future? You need to put mistakes behind you and look forward with determination and belief that today can be different. These are easy things to say, but difficult things to do. Start small.

Make your list of things to do, then focus on one item at a time. Put aside the fears and doubts that keep you from accomplishing your tasks. You don't need to be perfect. It is much better to do something less than perfectly than to do nothing but sit and fret. Spend one day working honestly on your list of things to do. Then sit down in the evening and notice your progress.

Assess your efforts and accomplishments frankly. You will know if you are hedging, so don't try to kid yourself.

Look for areas that might have been improved with a little more effort. Commit yourself to better performance. Vow to follow through on the projects you started. They are important. If you decide otherwise, be careful to make that decision with some gravity. The residue of uncompleted tasks can seriously diminish your self-esteem. However, if the project truly is not important, discontinue your work on it. Move on to something more meaningful. Something you have selected with care.

Once again, commit yourself and concentrate your efforts. You will find in time that you can turn the frustration of "So much to do; so little done" into the satisfaction of "So much to do; so much already done."

Giving In Gracefully

Acquiescence is the art of saying yes in situations where we might prefer to holler NO! or at least remain inconspicuously silent.

Acquiescence is practiced everywhere by all sorts of people. We see it on the job, in a marriage, in the classroom, on the public stage. We all acquiesce, but let us be reminded that acquiescence is an art.

Acquiescence is not a wholesale capitulation to another's position. That's called selling out. Nor is acquiescence a nod of the head with denial blazing from the eyeballs. That's playing at agreement and nobody is fooled by it. Acquiescence is subtler than either of these methods. Acquiescence involves a more dignified submission after expressing one's opposition in a rational way. It can also occur, however, without stating your opposition. In this case, you simply keep your argument to yourself.

There is something about the word acquiescence that bothers me. It reminds me of the word queasy, that feeling of being sick to your stomach. Nauseated. I hesitate to say that acquiescence is a bad word because we do need graceful surrenderers every now and then. But if acquiescence produces queasiness, watch out. You are violating your integrity and self-respect. You may feel you are preventing an embarrassing confrontation, but you are the victim of such an event.

Express your views honestly and sincerely. If you have strong feelings, stick to your guns. If the situation or topic is not crucial to you, then be gracious. Acquiesce. But please, don't be queasy.

Help for "Those Days"

A re you a scrambler? Can you pick up the pieces of an absurdly disrupted day, put them into a receptacle and carry them until tomorrow when you can reassemble them into some kind of order? Can you, when in a state of confusion, sidestep further trouble and aggravation long enough to get through the day?

Successful scramblers possess a variety of characteristics, including a sense of humor, patience, a sense of perspective and an optimistic outlook that says that for each troublesome day another day full of sunshine and joy awaits them.

We know that we get out of life what we put into it and that hard work and persistence pay off in accomplished goals. We can take the same attitude toward bad days and hardship in general. If you can get through the tough times, the good times are sure to follow.

When the day begins with an upsetting mishap do you shrug it off and go on? You will if you keep your eyes focused on the things you want to accomplish instead of brooding over the mishap and how it changed your plans. Think of the early morning spilled coffee on your skirt as an example. It's a curve ball for sure, but it's a fleeting thing.

When several things go wrong on the same day, do you unravel, throw your hands up in despair and vent your frustration on whoever happens to be nearby? We all know from experience that every now and then a particular day will seem to be marked for disaster. The best way to handle such days is to relax and accept them good-naturedly. Mamma said there'd be days like this! Do what you can and leave the rest for tomorrow, always believing that tomorrow will be better.

To become a successful scrambler, you need to cultivate a sense of humor, keep things in perspective and practice relaxing during times of stress. A positive attitude is essential, too. To develop a strong positive outlook, practice this exercise. When you recount (as we all tend to do) all the bad or sad things that have come your way over time, make sure you also list the good or happy things that have happened during that same time. Write them down. Study both lists. Then, throw away the bad list and keep the good one.

Recognize that even in the midst of disaster, some good exists. As you scramble through those horrible, nothing-is-going-right days, remember that something somewhere is quietly going right. Remember, too, that many days of promise lie ahead.

How to Be Taken Seriously

I wish there was a more elegant way to introduce this topic. There isn't. Not being taken seriously is a complaint I hear often.

Women today have a lot of jobs at work, home, school, church, and throughout the community. I suppose it is inevitable that somewhere along the way you will encounter someone who doesn't take you seriously. When it happens occasionally but not often, you can ignore the slight.

But when kids don't listen, spouses or partners don't respond, bosses don't hear you, and friends talk over the top of you when you really need some advice, it can get frustrating indeed.

What can you do to encourage others to take you more seriously?

Quit complaining. Listen to yourself for a day or two. Are you constantly running through your list of woes hoping for attention, sympathy or help? If nothing is right in your world and you are a broken record, what's to take seriously?

Create a plan. Kids won't help around the house? Create an age-appropriate task list and post it on the fridge with deadlines. When the work is done, distribute rewards. Notice results trigger rewards, not good intentions or feeble effort.

Get started. We all know someone who talks a great game about what she is going to do. After the third or fourth time, we tune out. After the seventh or eighth time, we start to feel embarrassed for her. She gets mad because nobody takes her seriously. If this is you, quit talking and get started. Every tiny step takes you closer to results.

Show results. Whether it is deadlines met, pounds lost, or money raised, when you can show progress, you put yourself into a different, more credible camp. Remember, little steps count.

Enlist help. While you may be incredibly gifted at multi-tasking, no one is entirely self-sufficient. Too many women move at the speed of light until they drop in exhaustion. Then they complain that nobody ever helps. Not surprisingly, their complaints fall on deaf ears. Why? Because people who know them expect that after a brief rest, these women will be right back doing it all.

Break the cycle. Ask for help and be specific. Whether it's compiling data, folding towels, or scheduling appointments, find easy ways for others to get involved.

Several years ago, I had the privilege of working with Mrs. Lim, a principal in a school in Brunei. Brunei is a tiny Muslim country along the South China Sea; I was part of a global team working to help school leaders transform their education system. During a Q&A session with the Minister of Education, Mrs. Lim stood up and asked what financial help the Minister could give her in order to build a library and an arts center at her school.

The Minister visibly scoffed at her question and asked why she expected him to take responsibility for her work. Mrs. Lim was struck dumb by the dismissiveness of his answer and my heart sank as I watched the color drain from her face.

For the next week, we spoke daily about the incident. At first Mrs. Lim railed against her humiliation. How dare the Minister be so rude? How foolish of her to risk becoming a public spectacle! She should have known better than to make such a request. Several days later, however, she began to consider his words more objectively. Although he had been abrupt in his response, she recognized his challenge and she responded to it.

When Mrs. Lim accepted a hefty check and congratulations from the Minister several months later, she proudly gave credit to her teachers and students. Quietly, she told me how wonderful it felt to be taken seriously.

How To Work for a Jerk

"You can choose your friends, but you can't choose your family." How often have you heard this when complaining about a pain-in-the-neck relative? In the same way, you can choose your job but you can't necessarily choose your boss.

Bosses, as a category, have a bad rep. Because they are bosses, people assume they are jerks. Many are not, but sadly those are the ones we don't hear much about. The jerks are the ones who get all the time over drinks during happy hour, dinner at home, and coffee each morning. By the way, a jerk is a jerk whether clad in a shirt and tie or a skirt and heels.

How can you make the best of a bad situation if you find yourself working for a jerk?

First, get your mind clear about the situation. It is not a life sentence, it is not unbearable, and it is not about you. Learning to take each day as it comes, realizing that even unpleasant days are filled with information can help curb the pessimism jerks tend to create. The faster you learn, the sooner you can reach for the next opportunity. If your boss is a jerk, chances are he didn't suddenly get that way when you started to work for him. You did not trigger his bad behavior and you are not responsible for it.

Second, learn to establish boundaries. You are not obliged to endure abusive behavior. You have the freedom to remove yourself from ugly situations. Learning to excuse yourself will take practice and some measure of courage initially. Be respectful, but be firm. You are not paid to be a whipping post.

If your boss criticizes you for lack of engagement, calmly point out that there are things she does which cause you to not think clearly or well. At these times you feel you add little value to a discussion. You may choose to state in specific terms the behavior you find objection-able—a loud voice or aggressive posture, for example—and let her know that when it occurs you will remove yourself from the situation.

This takes a calm heart and a level head, but it is doable. Role-play with a colleague to get comfortable. Be consistent and persistent. Your boss may learn to respect you for firmly drawing and maintaining your boundaries. Be aware that this can take a significant amount of time and effort, so don't expect immediate results or a miraculous turnaround in your boss's behavior.

Another technique that works is to calmly engage your boss by saying something like, "I see that you're upset. I'd like to help resolve the situation."

Don't offer a suggestion beyond these words. Let your boss take it from there. If she winds back up into a frenzy, stand or sit quietly until she finishes. Then repeat the two sentences. Your refusal to become upset or to take ownership of something that may not be your responsi-bility will eventually break through.

Third, watch how a jerk gets results. Because he is typically focused on the bottom line or his own ego, he will be oblivious to the impact his behavior has on morale. If pushed on the morale question, he will remind you that he is not paid to make workers happy, he is paid to deliver results. Bad behavior is thus justified in the name of productivity and profitability. While unfortunate and ill informed, this is the current reality in many organizations. Don't take it personally. And remember that learning what not to do can be a crash course in learning how to be more effective. Capture the lessons and use them to your advantage.

Finally, maintain your focus on the job and hold firm to your personal standards of courtesy, decency, and professionalism. The fact that your boss is a jerk has nothing to do with you. He will be that way whether you work for him or not. What matters is who you become and the type of boss you turn out to be.

It's Your Turn!

nother new year has arrived and with it a host of opportunities to make your life the way you want it to be. New starts are awesome! I remember as a kid the incredible emotions surrounding the first day of a new school year. I felt nervous about meeting the new teacher. What if she was mean? What if she was a really hard grader? What if she liked boys better than girls? Yes, I actually worried about that.

I also felt excited about learning so many new things. I was scared sometimes that I might not do well, but mostly I was eager to discover. And the start of each year brought interesting new kids into the classroom. Oh, how my heart leapt when Patrick joined our fifth grade class!

Life has moved on since then, with new starts marking the way. Some have been welcomed, even anticipated. Others represent unintended consequences of bad choices I made; still others were thrust upon me. I'm quite certain the same has been true for you.

What's on the horizon for this year? Smaller, more fuel-efficient cars. A new "Ribbon" interface for AutoCAD users. Discounted season passes at Sun Valley Ski Resort in Idaho. Sheer and see-through fabrics, fringed dresses, single-shouldered Grecian looks. Butterflies and bold, elegant jewel-encrusted clothing. Ripped jeans. "Statement" jewelry. Hairstyle extremes from pixie crops to milkmaid braids.

What will you choose for your life this year? What influences will you heed? Will you follow trends or break your own path? These are difficult questions for many women to answer. And because they are challenging, they are often ignored. Please don't do that.

Stop for a minute to consider what's next. Is there something in your life that you secretly yearn to do but feels nearly impossible? What if you could do it? What would change for you? When you feel absolutely at the top of your game, what makes you feel that way?

Go face yourself in the mirror. Smile as if something absolutely delights you. What do your eyes look like? What's happening inside? Do you feel a little surge of energy? Notice all these things; you'll want to create them for yourself.

Now put yourself in a foul mood. How do your eyes look? What's happening inside? Do you feel heavy? Does your stomach hurt? What else are you feeling?

Notice these things, too. They are what you want to eliminate.

Isn't it amazing how you can make your body feel strong or weak just by paying attention to your mood? It's even more amazing to realize that you can literally choose how to feel. I know that's an uncomfortable thought. Who wants to feel angry on purpose? Who wants to feel heavy and dull and sick?

Here's the challenge for this year. Practice being delighted. Practice making yourself feel strong. Shut out the things that put you in a foul mood. Forget about what other people are saying or doing. It's your turn to pursue the happiness you so desire. Take it. Run with it. No, it will not be easy. Don't expect unequivocal support. But don't get derailed by people who doubt. Make this the year that great things really do happen for you and for those you care about.

Remember that nothing miraculous happens overnight. Don't get discouraged when things are not substantially different by next Tuesday at noon. Take each day as the opportunity it is. When dark days descend—as they always do—put a brave smile on your face, turn out the lights, and tuck yourself in for some much-needed rest. Yes, I know that sounds impossible. Do it anyway. You might teach others in your household how to care for themselves.

Just like that first day of a new school year, the beginning of a new calendar year is a perfect inflection point. Turn things to your favor by intentionally practicing one little thing each day that will lighten your load, cheer your spirit, and make yourself proud. It's your turn.

Keep Track of the Dots

Throughout the crazy year that was 2011, women told me that, although they know how important it is to connect life's dots, they are simply too busy to do so. More telling was the wry question, "Dots? What dots?" Seems fewer and fewer of us have time to notice the dots, much less connect them.

Herein lies an invisible problem that is the source of some very real disappointment and fatigue, especially for women.

Women tend to be the keepers of the social fabric, ministering to the needs of family and friends. When I watch my daughters gently care for sick children and listen to Mom talk about managing Dad, who is suffering advancing Alzheimer's, I am inspired by their strength and heartened by their patience. And I know how life screams by while you are taking care.

Professional women juggle increasing numbers of balls while they work to advance in their careers. Job challenges, relationship issues, family worries, health concerns—there is so much that calls for attention, it is easy to feel like a pinball, bouncing from one situation to another. Looking back, it can be hard to see the sense of it all.

That is why it is important to keep track of your life. What dots are happening?

Journaling is a powerful means of self-discovery and learning, but many women resist the practice, feeling it is too time consuming or inconsequential. If you approach journaling as a "Dear Diary" exercise, you may quickly reach this conclusion. But I'd like to suggest a simple cataloging of events as an alternative.

Find a notebook, personal journal, or smart phone app that is easy to carry with you.

Then, whether you make time throughout each day, at the end of a day, or as a weekly practice, here are four items to track—four sets of dots, if you will.

1. Something you heard. Whether it is a fragment of conversation, the sound of wind through pine trees, the tenor of a child's cry, the pitch of your car's engine on a cold day, a favorite song, or the reassurance in a loved one's voice, jot down something you heard today. Do not judge it good or bad, useful or frivolous, meaningful or not. Just capture it.

2. Something you notice. In the same way, things you notice may not make sense; they may not appear to have any meaning at all. But when something captures your attention, jot it down. I saw a purple car the other day and noticed a penny in the street. Neither was the least bit important, but I wrote them in my journal because they caught my eye. When something captures your attention, capture it.

3. Something you learned. These are the ah-ha moments that happen in the shower, while you're driving to work, or as you listen to the tirade of a friend and have a sudden insight about the rant. When you realize something, no matter how trivial—or how late in the game—jot it down.

4. What you are thinking about now. This one is especially enlightening as you look back over your journal. What you think about day to day may be remarkably changeable and rich in what it can teach you.

By capturing the moments, events, and insights of your life at the time they occur, you are accumulating rich data about you, your life, and the dreams you are pursuing. What an amazing treasure chest of dots to consider! Taking time to notice life raises your energy level and gives you a sense of possibility. The real fun and value, however, come when you connect these dots to discover your life. This simple process can be a powerful catalyst for change, especially when you reach the cross-roads that beg for important decisions.

Managing Disappointment

Disappointment: It's everywhere. And sometimes I think women are especially attuned to it. Heaven knows we have our reasons.

Face creams that don't erase wrinkles as promised. Expensive gym memberships that don't make us divas. Spoiled produce. Stale bread. Bad gas mileage. Friends and family—family!—who don't get it.

Clothes that shrink. Computers that crash. Promises that are broken. Years that fly by without noticing the dreams we once had.

Disappointment is an everyday fact of life. I remember sitting on the back porch of a dear friend's house many years ago. I was pondering divorce and she was a single mom with two sons. She told me two things. "If you can find a way to say married, stay married. It's easier than being a single parent." I couldn't find a way to stay married.

The second thing she told me was, "If you can get used to the idea that everyone in your life—everyone in your life—will disappoint you at some time, you'll be able to handle just about anything."

We had a lengthy conversation about this. I didn't understand what she meant. I could not imagine how certain people in my life could ever disappoint me. It hurt just thinking they might. What I came to understand then, and have experienced many times since, is that people don't deliberately set out to disappoint you. But because they are human and they do what they do, at some point they will disappoint you in some way.

Teenage kids leave wads of used chewing gum on the edge of the counter top with the trashcan centimeters away. Friends go on and on about their current dramas, never asking how you are. Bosses accept truly outstanding work you produced on your own time without so much as an acknowledgment, never mind a thank you.

As I worked to complete this book, I watched the Green Bay Packers lose to the New York Giants in a Divisional playoff game. Again. I have been a Packers fan since I was a kid, when guys like Jerry Kramer, Boyd Dollar, Carroll Dale, Bart Star, Donny Anderson, Paul Hornung, Ray Nitschke, Elijah Pitts, and Bobby Jeter were my heroes.

The team went through a terrible trough for years. After beating all odds in 2010 to win on the road throughout the playoffs, make it to the Super Bowl and then win it, the expectations on the team the next year were sky high. And for the most part, the team responded, winning 15 games and losing only one all season.

But the team's performance in the playoff game was pathetic. Dropped passes, turnovers, even favorable calls by the referees could not secure a win for the home team. I speak for Packer Nation when I say the disappointment was bitter. *Bitter!*

The story I told myself about the Packers loss is important. "This loss is epic! It should not have happened! This team is bigger than their mistakes! They are steeped in character! They should have pulled together, focused their efforts, and done what they know how to do."

And what they are paid handsomely to do, I might add. The story I told myself about this disappointment made me deeply unhappy!

Yet I, and countless Packers fans across the nation and around the world, had no opportunity to influence the outcome.

I suspect your life is similar. Surely, there are parts that make you shake your fist in fury or your head in sadness. Disappointment stings. Just as surely, there are parts of your life that make you smile all the way to your toes. The stories you choose to tell yourself will either strengthen you or make you bitter and fragile. Women of beauty and substance choose stories that build and reject stories that diminish. It is a choice, though not an easy one.

Mischief is Good

What does mischief look like to you? A twinkle in an eye? A light-hearted shuffle step? A suppressed giggle in a semi-serious setting?

Mischief is good clean fun that falls over on the naughty side. Mischief is akin to inappropriate behavior. Mischief can certainly be unprofessional.

But mischief is refreshing. Mischief is uplifting. (To the mischief-maker, that is. It's a real pain in the neck to the one on the receiving end.)

I worked with a practical joker for a number of years. Every now and then, I would find my desk drawers stuffed with shredded paper. Once in a while, my phone would be duck taped to the desk. I retaliated with piles of peanut M&Ms on his office chair, which went flying when he yanked the chair out to sit down.

Mischief is part of our American heritage—pigtails dipped in inkwells; spitballs fired at classmates; britches torn on fences that weren't supposed to be climbed over.

It's really a shame that America has become such a grim and sober nation. Granted, we have much to be grim and sober about, and serious matters are not to be made light of. It is important for us to be serious, professional and self-possessed. But it is equally important to cultivate a little bit of mischief somewhere in our personalities. It helps keep the balance, you know.

Never Too Late to Start Over

Have you ever had the kind of day that makes you wish you could go back to bed and start over? Most of us have. On those days, it is sometimes best to finish it quickly and turn off the lights, vowing to make tomorrow better. However, it is also good to remember that it's never too late to start the day over. I have a large sign with these words hanging in my kitchen as a reminder to take a deep breath and start fresh.

Here are some suggestions that may help as well:

- Seek happiness in doing rather than in having.

- Increase your knowledge by listening more and talking less.

- Practice patience—even when you're tired.

- Let go of your concern for perfection.

- Ban the words "If only..." from your thinking. Replace them with the words "Today I will..."

- Learn contentment with who you are and where you are, despite what you feel you do not have.

- Approach problems sensibly and patiently. To help you do this, recall past difficulties that seemed insurmountable and remember how you overcame them.

- Cultivate a sense of humor.

- Take pride in your work; vow to turn in an honest day's work instead of agitating for a bigger title and fatter paycheck.

- Appreciate your family and friends. They are complex individuals, just like you.

- Get enough rest. Lost sleep makes you less logical and less effective. Give your best effort to your projects each day then set them aside until tomorrow.

- Exercise to maintain your health and to feel fit and strong. Avoid becoming preoccupied with sculpting the perfect figure.

- Banish one junk food item from your diet. If the results prove positive, get rid of another.

- Strive to make everyone who comes into contact with you feel comfortable and welcome.

- Use this day to make life better for someone you love. Keep in mind that happiness is like a boomerang. As you pass it out to others, it tends to come back to you.

Opportunity. Next Right.

You're cruising in the fast lane of life, listening to the radio, thinking about what you'll do when you get to wherever it is you are going. Just ahead a sign says: Opportunity. Next Right.

You smile a little when you see it and think, "That's nice." Then you motor right on by the next exit, looking briefly to the right and giving a quick nod to acknowledge that yep, that was opportunity.

We do it all the time. Why don't we stop? Or at least take a quick detour to check it out?

There are an infinite number of personal reasons, but some of the more universal ones might sound like this:

I don't have time. I have to reach my destination by 2:00.
That opportunity wasn't meant for me. It belongs to someone else.
I don't want to be distracted. I'm concentrating on something very important right now.

More honestly: *I'm scared. I don't have the confidence I need.*

Less astutely: *What opportunity?*

You know, of course, that it's up to you to find opportunity. It's not fate, it's not luck, and it is not being in the right place at the right time that is going to magically produce all kinds of tremendous opportunities.

You've got to train yourself to watch for the signs on the road. When you see them, stop the car. Get out and nose around. Ask questions. Probe for possibilities.

You might find a better way to get to where you were going in the first place. You might open up entire new areas of interest. At the very least, you will have broken the monotony of traveling through life on automatic cruise control.

Rebuild Your Confidence

*H*as your confidence been shaken by all the doom and gloom of recent years? Join the club. Everywhere I go, I see people with a look of uncertainty in their eyes as they try to make sense of what is happening around them.

But I also see people who have a flicker of defiance in their gaze. It's a look that says, "I don't know exactly what I'm going to do, but this struggle is for the birds." These people make me smile because they are ready to get moving.

I don't mean they are ready to take up arms or agitate crowds or picket for one reason or another. I mean they are realizing that despite systems and conditions that seem to control more and more of their daily lives, they have choices to make and energy to invest in creating a better future for themselves and their loved ones.

This energy is precious. And you have it, too. Here are some simple ways to harness energy to rebuild your flagging confidence.

First, recognize that even in the darkest of moments, you can choose to be strong. Franklin Delano Roosevelt (FDR), America's president from 1933 to 1945, asserted in his first inaugural speech that, "the only thing to fear is fear itself." This is an important reminder!

Fear steals your energy, prevents you from finding solutions, and invites you to be angry at something or someone whose decisions have caused you hardship. I'm sure you have felt this—we all have at one point or another.

Facing this fear and acting in spite of it is called courage. You have undoubtedly conquered fear at some point in your life, maybe many times. Learning to ride a bicycle or drive a car, starting a new job, going out on a date, working through conflict with a loved one—heck even trying a new hairdo can feel scary! Reflect on all the times you have triumphed over fear; they stand as proof of your capability and resilience.

Next, turn off negative inputs and, to the extent that you can, stay away from negative people. The old computer cliché is true for your mind, too: Garbage in, garbage out.

Fill your mind and spirit with uplifting information. Take time each day to absorb encouraging material, whether it is scriptures, biographies of great leaders, or timeless comedy. Restoring confidence is a lot like improving physical fitness. It must be intentional, disciplined, and continuous.

Another way to rebuild confidence is to keep track of things you do well. This may feel strange at first, especially if you were taught to be humble. For many of us, "Don't be conceited" was a mantra from our mothers. But making note of a well-prepared report, a perfectly aimed tennis serve, a happy child, or a sparkling clean kitchen gives you a sense of pride that nourishes self-confidence.

In the same way, keep a running list of things you notice. This practice helps you investigate the world around you, expecting something of interest to capture your attention. It sharpens your mind and stimulates your senses. It also makes YOU look different. Your eyes are clearer; your gaze is more engaged. You look interesting!

Finally, appreciate the goodness in your life. A sweet peach, the wag of a dog's tail, an email from a friend, your favorite song on the radio, a crystal clear blue sky, the sound of laughter from a loved one... these and a million other mini-miracles surround you every day. Take sustenance from them while you consider what's next on life's journey.

As you work quietly and purposely to rebuild your confidence, you may begin to notice that you affect others. Nelson Mandela, former president of South Africa and renowned world leader once said, "When we are liberated from our own fear, our presence automatically liberates others." By showing up to be you, you give others permission to do the same. As you rebuild your confidence, you teach others how to rebuild theirs. Now doesn't that beat a pity party, any day?

Stretchy You!

*P*eople are like rubber bands. They bend, they stretch, they come in a variety of shapes and sizes and colors. Some have great tensile strength; others snap at the slightest tug.

Rubber bands perform a variety of tasks—from holding articles together to propelling spitballs and opening stuck jar lids. People, too, have many talents that are not always apparent. But the most amazing similarity between people and rubber bands is the ability to expand.

As more things are added to a bundle, a rubber band expands to accommodate them. It never knows it can expand further until it actually does. We are, of course, "stretching it" by talking about what a rubber band knows or doesn't know, but the principle is important. In many instances, we don't know how much we can expand unless we actually try to or, as is more often the case, unless we are compelled to.

But sometimes people, like rubber bands, reach their breaking point. This can be the result of continuous stress or it can be triggered by a particularly traumatic event. The remarkable thing about people is that in due time following the snap, they simply tie little repair knots and carry on with life. Not the same as they were, perhaps, but here people have one up on rubber bands.

Once a rubber band has been broken and re-tied, it is untrustworthy. Not so with people. A mended break often makes for a stronger whole. What exactly is your limit? How far can you expand? This is not an invitation to fill up spare fat cells or see how big a belt you can grow into. Rather, it is an enticement to get you thinking about how you can grow in your outlook, your interests, and your daily activities.

Think of yourself as a rubber band. Are you a tiny, rigid one—the kind that has a nasty little sting when it breaks? Or are you one of those big, wide, hefty ones—the kind that seems to stretch forever and still have room for more?

The Cure for Inertia

*I*nertia, scientifically defined, means in part, the reluctance of a body to change its state of rest. This state of inertia is the exact opposite of and main impediment to momentum.

I like to imagine that inertia prompted the invention of the electric cattle prod, the alarm clock, and the nagging spouse.

Every human being who ever lived knows all about inertia, about being stuck in a state of "rest." We can laugh at it, make excuses for it, or avoid it like the plague, but inertia is definitely a force to be reckoned with.

Inertia often follows the disruption of a normal routine. If our momentum is checked in any significant way, it can become very difficult to get back on a roll. We may experience an illness, a business setback or the loss of a friend. Sometimes a series of minor accidents can alter our attitude to one of suspicion or apprehension, thus impeding our progress. Occasionally, we run across a dry spell in our lives during which our creativity is shot, our relationships are unsatisfying, and the procession of days seems meaningless. Inertia can also be the result, oddly enough, of trying too hard.

What is the cure for inertia? Sometimes support, understanding and encouragement from others is enough to get us going again. Sometimes professional help is necessary. And sometimes it seems that only the electric cattle prod will do the trick.

One good way to combat inertia is to relax and simply accept the fact that it gets everyone now and then. Try to stay active, try to remain open to others and keep a positive outlook. If you can, think of your period of inertia as a mental and emotional resting time. Learn to use it to re-evaluate your goals and activities. Maybe a reordering of your priorities is necessary. Remember, above all, that the dry spell will pass, inertia will be overcome, and sooner or later you will regain your momentum.

The Year of Confidence

Welcome to 20___! What kind of year will it be, you wonder?

"Why not shape it to your liking?"

"Ah, but that would take confidence."

"Yes, it would."

You can always tell when a woman has confidence. She is poised, relaxed, and open to others. She speaks simply and directly, laughs easily, and listens with interest. She makes decisions carefully, aware of the impact they may have on others. She encourages alternative viewpoints and engages in exploration of new ideas. A confident woman feels safe to be around.

Contrast this with the harried, uncertain, and guarded demeanor we all detest. Which woman are you?

Life's challenges have been unusually difficult in recent years. You may have been pressured in unfamiliar, even extreme, ways. Yet, if you reflect on the adversity you have managed, I'll bet you will find accomplishments. These victories, no matter how small, represent the seeds of confidence.

As you begin a new life chapter in 20___, why not make it one of purposeful development and improved confidence. How?

First, pay attention to the things you believe and care about. We live in a noisy world of experts who like to tell us what is true and right. But experts disagree with one another and they do not necessarily understand your world. Listen with a grain of salt, being mindful of bias—theirs and yours.

Next, identify special gifts you have, be they skills, talents, connections, or attitudes. Think about how you would like to develop and use your gifts in the New Year.

You may have learned to be hesitant in this regard. Many women are. If you listen to the ways women are discouraged from developing and sharing their gifts, you may hear things like, "She thinks she is so much better than everybody else." "She doesn't know what she is talking about." "She is not as good as she thinks she is." "She is aggressive."

None of this is useful feedback, yet many women take it to heart, feel deficient, and stop contributing altogether, or try harder to appear competent. Neither strategy leads to improved confidence. What does?

Do not compare yourself to others. When you do, you may begin to feel anxious or resentful on one hand or smug on the other hand. You are like no one else; why try to be like someone else?

Do not compete. Using the accomplishments of others as benchmarks for yourself is another recipe for frustration or complacency. Set your goals and decide on the measuring stick you will use to calculate your progress.

Identify a talent you have, whatever it might be. Do not worry about whether it is something you can exploit financially. The world we live in today uses money as its primary yardstick. "If you do not make a pile of money," it says, "you are not successful." Baloney.

You might be the best listener in your circle of friends, the one everyone seeks out to air complaints, think through challenges, and find workable solutions. If you are a therapist, you may be paid handsomely for this gift. If, like many good listeners I know you are not a therapist, please do not diminish the value of your gift. Lives have been saved when friends cared enough to listen.

Perhaps you make people laugh. Maybe you have an amazing voice. Your homemade greeting cards are works of art. You make killer brownies. You can (still) do cartwheels on the lawn with grandchildren. Your flair for fashion draws admiring glances. Your patience and good humor in the face of illness helps others count their blessings.

The ways you touch and inspire the world are unique to you. Make this the year you focus on the talents you want to develop and the contributions you want to make. Our communities are hungry for your gifts. Your friends love to see you smile and laugh. When you commit yourself to growing in ways that matter to you, your confidence soars. At the same time, you show other women how to be fabulous! That's a New Year's gift we can all embrace.

To Sleep or Not to Sleep?

ometimes we find unexpected humor in the everyday, mundane, taken-for-granted things of life. Take, for instance, this observation: "Bed is a bundle of paradoxes. We got to it with reluctance, yet we quit it with regret; and we make up our minds every night to leave it early, but we make up our bodies every morning to keep it late."

Everyone knows how this feels. Some accept the fact that the mind is willing but the body is weak. Others, however, curse their humanness even as their eyelids drift shut after the alarm clock is silenced.

We make big plans, don't we? And we make lists and map long-range plans of action. Sometimes, though, we list so many things to do that we don't know where to begin. We struggle all day with decisions and by nighttime, we long for the comfort of our beds.

Once there, we lie awake second-guessing the day's actions and establishing criteria for tomorrow's decisions. Eventually, toward morning, exhaustion takes over and we succumb to sleep.

Then, almost instantly, the alarm rings, we groan at the morning and roll over for a few minutes more rest. It is only with great regret that we drag ourselves out. The scenario is different, of course, if we have something especially exciting or challenging to wake up to. In this case, we bound out of bed and hit the floor running, not to pause until fatigue tackles us. Sleep is a necessary evil that we fight morning and night.

Yes, bed is a paradox. It is the source of comfort and frustration. We can't do without it, but sometimes it interferes with our plans. Life is full of such paradoxes and we spend a lot of time defeating ourselves. If only we could screen out the distractions around us, concentrate on our goals, and be content with making daily progress instead of expecting instant results, we might then go happily to bed and wake willingly to take on the perplexities of the new day.

To Win Arguments, Don't Argue

How would you like to win every argument you get caught in from now on? You can if you're willing to change your idea of winning an argument. The first thing you must do is shut your mouth, shut off your arguments, put your thoughts in a closet and shut the door. Now your distractions are gone and you can listen to what's going on with the other guy. Be aware, of course, that your opponent will interpret this as surrender.

When you keep your mouth in motion and your thoughts churning behind it, you are in effect talking to yourself. Each thing you say is a small segment of your major theme. You listen for how it sounds and repeat or alter it to make your point stronger. And all the while you are doing this, your opponent is often doing the same. Thus, an argument appears to be a two-sided event, but in many cases it is simply two solo acts butting up against one another. Very little of one side is absorbed by the opposite side. No one is heard, nothing is learned, and chances are excellent that this same debate will run again at a later time.

If, however, you can tune in to the other guy and listen for a while, you may begin to see things differently. You might want to alter your position somewhat. Because you haven't previously roared out your opinion, you can now change your mind about the issue without embarrassment. You save face. You win. You may, in fact, learn something about the issue that you didn't know. That's education. You win. You may learn something about the other person—why he differs, where he is coming from, what his needs are, why he has to win. That's developing insight. You win. You may learn something about yourself and you will learn how to manage a difficult situation. That's self-discovery and growth. You win.

It is easy to talk about what we should do in a confrontation situation, but once we are embroiled in one, we tend to forget it all. Winning arguments this way is not easy. But you win in so many ways that even if you eventually lose the argument, you win.

Too Many Choices?
How to Make Up Your Mind

*I*sn't it exciting that today, like never before, you can have more, be more and do more with your life? *Carpe diem*, my friend! Seize the day!

Yes, well. It is certainly true that we have more choices than ever before. We are also reminded like never before to drink deeply from life's abundant fountain.

Yet there are times when the fountain feels like a fire hose. There is too much coming at us at a pace we find impossible to manage. How can we maintain some measure of composure while making life's choices?

It is an important question. For some perspective, let's look at how the world has changed for women. Just two-and-a-half generations ago, our mothers' lives were defined by social mores and restricted to a handful of traditional roles—daughter, wife, mother; maybe teacher or nurse. As always, a few mavericks challenged these roles but for the most part, women knew what was expected of them and generally sought to do well and find happiness within these boundaries. There simply wasn't much to choose from.

Beginning in the 1960s, women like Betty Friedan and Gloria Steinem said, "Wait a minute. There's more to women than their roles and more to life than staying at home." The agitation of the Women's Movement fomented major change in laws, economics and attitudes, which ultimately opened up new highways of opportunity for women.

Perhaps the greatest change that emerged over the years is the way in which women thought about themselves—the way in which each of us thinks of ourselves—in the context of families, jobs, and greater communities. Given the richness of opportunity and the nearly limitless nature of choice, many women today find themselves more stymied than liberated. We still bear the hangover of traditional expectations as we try to make up our minds.

Is it selfish to concentrate on creating my future before considering the desires or needs of others? Is it possible to keep everyone's needs and opinions in mind while making important choices? What if a good idea today turns into a disaster in coming years? What will people think about me if I choose this path or decline that opportunity? What if I end up alone?

Women are relationship oriented. This is a very good thing. Society would be lost without our attention and concern, and our lives would be quite hollow without family, friends and colleagues. However, we must avoid the trap of trying to guess what is good for everyone else in choosing what will bring meaning and satisfaction to our lives. We must also guard against placing too heavy an emphasis on other people's opinions.

The first rule—indeed, maybe the only rule—in making up your mind is "Think It Through."

- **Think.** This requires time and deliberate attention to a choice at hand. By definition it is not an emotional reaction or a frantic spinning of wheels.

- **It.** Can you clearly state the choice or decision you are trying to make? Often, "it" gets colored by fear of what others will think or say and becomes impossibly cloudy. When your vision gets fuzzy, your emotions sneak out to play.

- **Through.** Think all the way to the end. Imagine yourself embracing a successful choice. See how it benefits others because you are energized. Your happiness makes you more generous, patient and loving. The other seductive choices have been cleared away; they no longer consume your energy. This particular aspect of making a choice is critical. Too often we call a decision the thing that happens when we get sick of thinking about something. Then we act on this thing only to find ourselves face to face with the disappointing 'what if' question. If you are not ready to choose, give yourself more time.

Your life unfolds in chapters. Each one presents a menu of choices, but not every choice is appropriate for every chapter. You make up your mind to choose some things and reject others. This is perfectly natural and abidingly correct. You wouldn't eat hot fudge and sauerkraut at the same time, would you?

Transitions Bring Questions

*I*n addition to Mother's Day and Memorial Day, the month of May brings many special anniversaries. The Kentucky Derby was first run in 1875. The Red Cross was founded in 1881. The Ringling Brothers Circus opened in 1884. Masking tape was patented in 1930. The Golden Gate Bridge opened in 1937. Mount St. Helens erupted in 1980. The first photo was sent from the Hubble space telescope in 1990.

History shows us that May is a celebratory month of invention and transition. As we welcome the warmer days of May in Wisconsin, we know that many women around the state are considering or experiencing transition.

From celebrating birthdays to managing transitions of kids nearing graduation, personal career moves, changes in health or relationships, and the prospect of retirement, this May the times they are a' changing.

Life's journey is filled with change and transition, which in turn fills us with questions. What's next? What's possible? Is this the right decision? What if I'm wrong? What will my family and friends think? What should I say? What should I do? Who am I? Who am I now?

These questions can feel scary and confusing, especially if you try to answer them all at once. The question that's really on our minds is, "Will I be okay?"

If you face a transition that is new or unusual, you may question your ability to deal with it. But take a moment to consider all the transitions you have already successfully managed. You didn't know how to walk until you learned through trial and error. You didn't know how to communicate with others until you tried to share your ideas and figured out how to listen to theirs. You didn't know how to get through a time of grief until you lost a loved one.

You may recall a time when you were in the midst of a difficult transition thinking you might not make it through. But you did. And you will again.

The "Who am I?" and "Who am I now?" questions can be the most troubling and difficult to answer. Re-creating an identity when faced with significant change is often bewildering and painful. I have come to believe these questions prolong the struggle of transition and may be not only unproductive, but indeed harmful.

I believe this because I have talked with so many women over the years who wonder who they are when the job they have done for much of their adult lives comes to an end. They wonder who they are when their children leave home to begin shaping their own lives. They wonder who they are when a spouse dies or a partner leaves them. The "Who am I now?" question often feels shapeless and overwhelming.

And yet, you are still you even after losing a role identity. If you are like many women today, you have probably invested more time creating and living up to a particular role or set of roles, than discovering who the woman is who answers to your name.

A healthier set of questions at times of transition might include "What kind of person do I want to be?" "Given my talent and experience, where could I make a real contribution?" "What do I want to learn about next?"

These questions draw upon what you already know about yourself, what you know you could do if you really put your mind to it, and what you want to be remembered for. The energy that is created by thinking about these questions is positive. It encourages exploration and invites experimentation.

The questions we ask ourselves at times of transition have no immediate answers. This is a good thing. They force us to dig deeper and challenge us to find new pathways. The woman you discover along the way will be delightful. I promise.

The next time you face a transition—and you will—ask yourself what kind of person you want to be as you navigate the transition and as you begin the next chapter of your remarkable, one-of-a-kind life. Embrace the questions. Dare to live the answers.

What Will the Neighbors Think?

The largest single stumbling block to accomplishment is fear. Fear makes us procrastinators, quitters, and sticks-in-the-mud. Mankind has many fears, not all without cause. But the one fear that holds back more people than any other is the fear of what other people will think.

You know that fear. You've felt it a hundred times: When you commented favorably on a movie that someone else hated. When you made a decision at work that someone vigorously opposed. When you enjoyed a sport that someone scorned as silly child's play. When you wore new clothes, cut your hair, read a new book, sent a card, or cooked a meal. To the person who constantly wonders what kind of impression he or she is making, every action is agonizing.

Generally, you understand what others expect of you. You also have self-expectations, which are often higher, more demanding and more rigid than any that others might impose upon you. As you struggle to live up to the expectations of yourself and others, you may become alternately nervous, defensive, insecure and confused. You waste your time, your energy, your life.

Relax! Forget about what others might think of you. There is no one watching your every move. Most people are too concerned with what others think of them to spend time judging you. Ease up on your self-expectations. Learn to experience the joy of doing something for its own sake. Resist the urge to impress someone. Choose your lifestyle to reflect your unique personality. Be yourself openly and joyfully, uninhibited by the opinions of others. You may be surprised to find new appreciation in the eyes of others, and a new level of respect.

Woe Is Me!

For the "Ain't it awful" category: You have generously added ten pounds to your frame and though you struggle daily to lose it, you simply cannot. Every morning you wake up determined to make this the day you start your diet. The more you concentrate on not eating, the more aware you become of every tasty morsel in your house. You drool during Pizza Hut commercials. And at day's end, after eating absolutely everything you can find "for the last time," you vow to get serious tomorrow.

The scenario is familiar to many. Sometimes—on our better days—it is humorous. But anyone who has fought this particular fight knows how difficult it is to get started and how hard it is to sustain a positive attitude. Every bit of backsliding registers as failure. We condemn ourselves for being weak and undisciplined in addition to being fat. We begin to withdraw from others. We know our friends just wouldn't understand or worse, they would discover how disgusting we are. Our misery is complete... and real.

This sad situation occurs too often in our lives. The more we stare at a problem and brood over it, the more serious it becomes. We grow self-involved, anti-social and irritable. But the problem is neither solved nor dissolved by concentration or worry. Action is the answer.

But stop! Before taking action, forget about the problem. Forget about yourself. Take a two-week hiatus from your self-spun cocoon of misery. Spend time with friends, family and children. Talk over their problems, not yours. Play with them, care for them, get to know them better. After two weeks, look again at your troubles. Are they as crucial as you once thought? Perhaps you now see new solutions. In the case of the unwanted ten pounds, you may find that some have been lost.

The moral of the story? Put your stewing pot on the back burner and go see what others have cooking. You may find your troubles easier to live with.

Hidden Truths

We make our way through life looking for markers to reassure us we're on the right track and heading in a positive direction. But sometimes the biggest truths are hidden in the most innocent places. The key is to pay attention to what's before you and truly see what's there.

George Bernard Shaw, an Irish literary critic, playwright and essayist who won the Nobel Prize for Literature in 1925, wrote:

When a thing is funny, search for a hidden truth.

and

Life isn't about finding yourself. Life is about creating yourself.

A Lowly Power Position

Customer service is often perceived as an entry-level job that doesn't pay very well, carries a lot of stress, and suffers high turnover. In some cases, this perception is reality. But I'd like to offer a different idea: customer service is a power position!

Think about it. Who has the best view of how customers experience your business? Who sees sales trends long before reports come out? Who has the greatest in-the-moment influence over customer satisfaction? Customer service representatives, including retail checkout people and in-store service agents.

Businesses of all kinds spend incredible amounts of time, energy and money creating the right atmosphere for customers to be happy. They offer distinctive goods and services. They decorate retail outlets to induce purchasing behavior. They design websites that are exciting and user-friendly. They build brand awareness through high budget multimedia campaigns. Making a first impression that gets a customer to say "wow!" is a big deal.

How the customer exits an experience with the business can also create a "wow." This wow may be enthusiastic if the experience is consistent with exciting first impressions. It may be disappointed if the expectation is not met. Or it may be downright angry if the customer's actual experience is far different from the expectation that was created.

The way in which customer service people interact with clientele, how knowledgeable they are about products, services and policies, how attentive they are to customer questions or complaints, and how quickly and smoothly they respond to all requests determines this wow factor.

Here are some tips for excelling as a customer service power player:

- Adopt a friendly, businesslike manner. Listen to understand the full question or need, rather than assuming you know what it is after the customer's first few words. Be open. Recognize that a customer's issue is not about you and you have the opportunity to resolve it!

- Develop proficiency in using customer service tools: Telephones, computers, checkout machines, resource directories, contact information for additional help.

- Technical glitches are annoying for everyone. Your confidence in using all the tools available will help your customers feel cared for.

- Become familiar with every aspect of your company's business. Learn how products are made and from what materials. When you can tell a story about your products, you'll add a touch of intelligence and charm to your offerings.

- Pay attention to the ways in which your company sells product—in retail outlets, over the Internet, by phone, by mail order, or via sampling at special events. Understand what your customers look for in each of those venues.

♦ Study how customers make their purchases. Do they prefer to use cash or some form of credit? When they return your company's goods, what are the most common reasons? How easy is the return process? Is there an opportunity to offer your customers something that would suit them better? Your mission is to keep them in the customer fold.

♦ Observe the order entry process and pay attention to errors. Could the system be made easier to use? Are orders fulfilled correctly? Is there a notification process when items are out of stock?

♦ Create summary reports of what you hear and learn from your customers and share them with your boss. Consider a weekly email summary of key themes or a graph showing weekly customer activities.

Approaching customer service as a power position opens opportunities to leverage the role in multiple ways. The more you learn about your business and its customers, the more valuable an asset you become to your company. Can a promotion be far behind?

An Empty Bag and an Ax to Grind

*P*oor *Richard's Almanack,* a yearly almanac published by Benjamin Franklin from 1732 to 1758, is a delightful source of homey witticisms that strike at the truth of life in clever ways. Consider for instance, "It is hard for an empty bag to stand upright." There is no debating the surface truth of that statement, and if we look a little deeper, we find a commentary on man's character. It is difficult, we know, to stand tall without something to stand for.

To argue without facts is to fall on one's face. To profess love from a cold and barren heart is to feel wretched loneliness. There are many possible interpretations, but the general advice is to fill our minds and hearts and lives with strength and goodness. The resulting character will enable us to stand strong and sure in any circumstance.

Also from *Poor Richard's Almanack* comes this observation: "When I see a merchant over-polite to his customer, begging him to take a little brandy, and throwing his good on the counter, thinks I, that man has an ax to grind."

A chuckle escapes me as I envision this scene. Think of the many things you do in a day. How many are purely motivated and how many are done to achieve an effect or to obscure a true motive? Do you kill

---

others with kindness and choke on your own spite? Do you grin and shrug instead of confronting a problem? Are you an apple-polisher? Do you express admiration when you secretly abhor?

In the name of tact, we are guilty of some of these things. But our relations would be better served with a greater proportion of truth. We instinctively mistrust the squirrelly character—the one whose speech, actions, and facial expressions are out of synch.

Speak your truth plainly. Be honest with those who hurt you and appreciate those who make you laugh. Try always to express yourself with dignity and clarity. Your reward will be greater ease with others and fewer axes to grind.

Poor Richard's Almanack is full of old-fashioned, outdated gems. Isn't it fun to dig them out, dust them off, and find the hidden truths for today?

Are you 'The Real Deal'?

uthenticity is a beautiful thing. A powerful thing. Something that allows you to live the way you want to live, comfortable in your own skin. Authenticity is also very invitational. We like people who are genuine, trustworthy, and reliable.

Every woman I know would like to be comfortable in her own skin—to live authentically, peacefully, in harmony with man (figuratively) and nature. We women strive to be "the real deal."

But we're constantly bombarded with messages encouraging us to be better, stronger, prettier, more patient, more helpful, softer, more successful, more assertive, more, more, more. There's even a magazine called *More*, targeted to women over 40.

Here's a question that cracks me up and makes me uncertain: "Are you younger or older than you think?" Well, gosh, I hadn't thought about it. I think younger, but maybe this test will tell me otherwise. So am I comfortable in my own skin? I thought so, but maybe not. The ambivalence is corrosive.

The late Abraham Maslow is one of my favorite psychologists because he was so curious about how we humans think and act. He dedicated his life to studying successful human behavior (as opposed to studying illness) and wrote prolifically about the things that influence us. He developed a five-level "Hierarchy of Needs," asserting that all humans have similar needs, that these needs can be ordered in an ascending scale, and that until one level of need is met, the next level cannot be embraced.

His first level of need is Physiological, things such as food, water, and oxygen—survival stuff. Next come Safety needs, the things or conditions that make you feel unafraid. If you've ever had to struggle to meet these two levels of need, you understand how consuming they are.

The third level is Love and Belonging. This level is about the need to give and receive love, to have a sense of belonging somewhere. Internet dating sites are all about this.

Next come Esteem needs, which are about feeling valuable, having self-respect, and feeling the respect of others. Our overly commercialized society makes this one difficult.

At the top of Maslow's pyramid is Self-actualization, or authenticity. Maslow believed that this is the level at which you understand your calling, where "a musician must make music, an artist must paint, and a poet must write." He believed that very few people ever achieve this level and he postulated that social barriers were often the reason why.

This fascinates me. I think his theory explains, at least in part, why so many people feel frustrated, angry, or left out. e.e. cummings wrote "The hardest thing to do is to be yourself in a world trying to make you into someone else." Isn't that true?

Here's what I believe. We live life in chapters. Some are more challenging than others. Some are more satisfying than others. But the struggle and learning of each chapter makes us stronger. When we embrace and work through each chapter, we become more real.

Society wants to air-brush fine lines and battle scars; our culture wants to celebrate youth and potential. Having a forward-leaning orientation is good! The future is ours to make, after all. But erasing evidence of where we've been, what we've collected so far (be it pounds, lines, or something else) and what we've learned is a recipe for depression and regression. These are the things that mark our progress and give us distinction. We are unique because we experience life like no other and collect evidence of this experience as only we can. That's authenticity. That's something to celebrate.

So instead of trying to be like somebody else, I'd advocate reflecting on your personal experience with life. Listen to the stirrings inside yourself that point you in a direction only you can go. Present yourself with pride, knowing that some will understand you because they are on the same level as you, but others won't know who you are, what you represent, or what you're talking about because they're not there yet. That's about them, not you.

Yes, we need to adapt to environmental and cultural expectations. Diplomacy skills are useful in a pluralistic society. But you are here for a very brief time, you have things to contribute that no one else can, and no matter what stage or Level of Need you're working on, you're teaching others important things about yourself and our world today. That's authenticity.

Beautiful Eyes

An old English proverb says, "The eyes are windows to the soul." How true this is! And what profound meaning it carries as we think about how to make them more beautiful.

A friend of mine has had permanent eye cosmetic procedures, including permanent eyeliner and new eyebrows. She paid a pretty penny for each procedure and periodic touch-ups are required. She looks beautiful! Her confidence skyrocketed after each procedure and she is now thinking about wearing colored contact lenses.

I have noticed over the past several months, however, that my friend has become dispirited. The excitement and confidence she felt following her eye enhancements has worn off. She frets constantly about her finances, family, and job. She notices everything that is wrong with her life, while shrugging off any suggestion about what might be right with it. Her eyes are dull and tired. Windows to her soul, indeed.

While advances in cosmetology and technology can certainly help us appear more beautiful, the long-lasting secret to gorgeous eyes is to light them from within! Here are five no-cost suggestions for creating beautiful, alluring eyes.

1. **Pay attention**. Whether you are conversing with a friend, attending a meeting, serving a customer, or finding your way to a new location, paying keen attention engages your mind and imagination. Your eyes shine with alertness and interest.

2. **Be curious.** The fastest, most cost effective way to brighten tired eyes is to wonder about something and go in search of information. Curiosity opens the mind to exploration and discovery. Curious eyes open wider, too, and radiate energy.

3. **Practice appreciation**. Have you ever seen people's eyes soften when they see a puppy, a spectacular sunset, or a loved one? Appreciation makes eyes glow with happiness, serenity, and quiet joy. For beautiful eyes, find something in your world each day to appreciate. Make time to really see the things that are dear to you. Keep a notebook of these gifts to remind yourself—and soften your eyes—on blue days.

4. **Share laughter.** Next time you laugh with a friend, notice how her eyes sparkle. Watch a child laugh and you will see excitement and pure joy pour from his or her eyes. How contagious this is! And sadly, how rare it is becoming.
    Our world has grown colder, darker, and more somber as the worries of the past year have preoccupied us. You may feel sometimes that laughter is inappropriate, that it somehow belittles your concerns. But laughter keeps the soul fresh and the eyes animated. It makes people wonder what you're up to. This curiosity lights up their eyes, too.

5. **Engage with others.** Barbra Streisand famously sang, "People who need people are the luckiest people in the world." The happiest, too! Whether listening to others, appreciating idiosyncrasies, sharing insights, or telling stories, people who connect with others

look more alive. Their eyes shine with curiosity, sparkle with appreciation, and twinkle with humor.

These are basic, everyday practices that can, admittedly, seem too bland or too time-consuming to make any difference. It may seem easier to pay for newfangled procedures that promise remarkable beauty results.

But your eyes tell the world what is going on inside your heart and mind. No cosmetics, permanent or otherwise, can disguise pain, fear, or fatigue. That's an inside job that starts between your ears.

If you want eyes that sparkle and glow, take care of your health, get enough sleep, and get out into the world! Find things to be curious about. Seek new ideas. Call people you find interesting. Visit new places. Even gas stations and pharmacies can be as interesting as coffee shops and museums if you visit them with the right mindset. Pay attention to what's happening in your part of the world and be grateful for each new day.

I promise that if you embrace these five simple habits and practice them on purpose, your friends and colleagues will begin noticing something different about you. Don't be surprised if someone you have known a long time suddenly notices how beautiful your eyes are.

Commitment is Energizing

*H*ow times change as the years unfold. Things speed up, patience falls, mistakes get made faster, lessons are learned slower, and with each generation it seems that what was once valued goes out of style.

Commitment is one of the things that has taken a beating in recent decades. There was a time when kids poked their fingers with pins, squeezed out a drop of blood and joined fingertips to become blood brothers—friends for life.

Can you imagine such a practice in today's world of HIV and other blood borne diseases? Any kid who would become interested in the notion of blood brotherhood would have to execute the pact in deep secrecy and at the risk of severe sanction if caught. Sort of like the way sexual experimentation happened among teens once upon a time.

There was a time when loyalty was highly valued as a quality of character. In business, the pact between worker and employer was understood as a long-term promise of partnership unless and until an egregious act of malice or error provided indisputable reason for severance.

Those days are long gone. The convulsive economic expansion and contraction that has taken place in fits and starts over the past two decades has recast employment expectations. A recent Ipsos study found that one in five employees expressed loyalty to their current employer. This drops to just one in three in companies that have recently frozen wages or downsized.

People no longer expect to stay in any job for more than a few years and many don't want to. Workers in the IT industry are most transient, thanks in part to the rapid and constant change of technologies, but also due to the intellectual curiosity and restlessness of many in the industry.

On the social front, current divorce statistics in the United States range from 36 to 50 percent, depending on the source, with divorce rates among younger couples substantially higher than among their elders. The average length of a marriage that ultimately ends in divorce is roughly eight years.

Today's preoccupation with living in the moment, going for the gusto, and being all you can be makes it hard for the idea of commitment to gain any popularity. Why would we staple ourselves to something that might not work, after all? When something better comes along, we want to be free to grab the opportunity. Such windows open and close with incredible speed! No sense being hemmed in by a current responsibility.

So commitments you thought you made—to job, partner, career— didn't pan out. You feel bad. Maybe there's a twinge of guilt. Maybe it's irritation at having been pressured to say yes when all along you would have preferred to say no. Maybe it's genuine remorse because circumstances changed in ways you could not control.

Whatever the reason for breaking a commitment, the aftermath brings a feeling of letdown. Your sense of self takes a hit. Tiny disappointments add up over time to feelings of inadequacy, self-doubt and gloominess.

And you long for something more stable. More sure. More satisfying.

Something like commitment? Something that calls on the best of you; that requires careful consideration and thoughtful decision making? Commitment is a promise you make to yourself to do something that is important to you. When you make it with firm resolve, it becomes an animating force that serves to narrow your focus and direct your energies. The "live for today!" distractions that surround you fade in importance when you decide where you want to go.

Close your eyes. Envision yourself as happy and fulfilled. Make the decision to be that way. Now create a series of attainable goals—baby steps—to prove to yourself that you are capable of achievement. Notice your energy level. It feels good, doesn't it?

Tell yourself a strong story about commitment and feel the pride that comes with making a certain decision. As you fulfill your promise to yourself, you will find that you are acting with greater confidence and conviction. Protect your progress; it will be tender at first. But stay true and watch what happens. Commitment is energizing!

Criticism is like Champagne

Criticism, like mistakes, is a necessary ingredient to learning. It occurs daily in millions of situations, but it is often misguided, misunderstood and misused. Because of this, criticism has earned a bad name.

But consider what life would be like without criticism. For those in a position to criticize, it would mean keeping their knowledge and experience to themselves and leaving less experienced people to learn or not learn as chance permitted. In many instances, parents, teachers, bosses, clergymen, and professional critics of all kinds would be silenced.

For the criticized, it would mean one of two things: relief from unwanted or unnecessary instruction, or deprivation of truly helpful advice. Thus, children, students, subordinates and novices of every nature would gain peace or lose opportunities for improvement.

Criticism is a vital part of human interaction. As the criticized, we need the maturity to accept or reject gracefully what is offered.

As we encounter criticism, let's keep this thought in mind: "Criticism is like champagne—nothing more execrable if bad, nothing more excellent if good. If meager, muddy, vapid and sour, both are fit only to engender colic and wind; but if rich, generous and sparkling, they communicate a glow to the spirits, improve the taste, expand the heart, and are worthy of being introduced at the symposium of the gods." (Charles Caleb Colton).

Double Dog Dare

here are many recipes today for a happy and successful life. This kind of life is determined, I believe, just as much by one's attitude as it is by one's actions. With this in mind, here are a few suggestions to consider.

Use your head. It is popular knowledge that we humans use only about ten percent of our brains. (More recent research suggests a much smaller number; less than one percent!) This is a depressingly small percentage that hints at phenomenal potential. The equipment you carry around in your skull is incredible. Figure out a way to use it.

Look for new opportunities. They are out there and not just for your buddy or your brother. They are waiting for you as well. Get out of your chair, hitch up your drawers, open that door and go looking.

Put fear out of your life; it will only impede your success. Fear is responsible for doubt, mistrust and hatred. It weakens your resolve and encourages complacency once a safe spot is found. Replace fear with confidence and a spirit of adventure. Then watch yourself grow.

Concentrate on people. They are the foundation and substance of all our lives. Each person you meet carries into your life a fine strand. You interweave the strands of all the people you meet and the net result is your life. It can be rich and thickly braided, a beautiful life filled with human interaction. Or it can be flat and brittle and cold, a life lived mostly alone with singular goals and little influence from or upon others. Keep in mind that you are a "people" too, carrying your strand into the lives of others. It can be fun and growth producing to get "tangled up" with others.

Dare to be the you who only you can be. It's an old thought—a cliché by now—but if you understand what it means, I double dog dare you.

Gifts from Old Man Winter

A traveler's advisory is posted…roads are snow-covered and slippery…blowing and drifting snow…an additional two to four inches expected…

Old Man Winter came quickly this year, didn't he? Suddenly, after a beautiful, crisp, and sunny fall day, the clouds moved in, flurries turned into inch upon inch of accumulation and a characteristic winter gray settled over the landscape. The calendar shows early November. Boy, do we need some positive thoughts in a hurry!

Let's see. If you'd had your camera ready, you could have snapped a classic winter wonderland scene perfect (and in plenty of time) for your Christmas greeting cards.

Winter is quiet. There are no squealing tires racing through the neighborhood. Winter is fragrant. Pine trees, wood-burning stoves, and homes warm with hearty winter meals give this season a special aroma all its own.

Kids love winter. It is the only season they can romp outside all day, flinging their little bodies to the ground without fear of serious harm, and come in to a warm house and steaming mugs of hot chocolate crowned with miniature marshmallows. They look forward to each new snowfall, too, because it comes with the possibility of a snow day—no school!

Fitness minded people can rejoice in winter. There are all kinds of outdoor sports to challenge them including skiing, skating, hockey, snow football, snowshoeing, ice sailing and bobsledding—not to mention the great workout provided by snow shoveling.

For those less athletically inclined, winter affords the perfect excuse for curling up in a chair or stretching out on the sofa to read, ponder and plan for better days.

And, of course, one of the best things about winter is the holiday. We have Thanksgiving, a time to reflect upon and give thanks for our many, many blessings; Christmas, a time of peace, joy and hope; and New Year's, a time of anticipation and heightened resolve.

Winter, despite its inconveniences, its sloppy weather, and its gray pall, does have its good points. Find them and hold fast until the first glimmers of spring!

Give Thanks for Difficulty

would like to encourage you to write a thank you note today. Begin by saying thank you for obvious things: family, friends, home, health, occupation and wealth. Express gratitude for your physical capabilities, your ability to communicate with others and your gift of choice.

Don't forget the rare beauty of a quiet moment, the refreshment of a steamy shower on a chilly morning, and the abundance of nourishing food. It is not difficult to be thankful for the many good things you enjoy.

Now I want you to say thank you for the less obvious things: physical shortcomings, financial setbacks, and problems of all kinds. Why should you give thanks for problems? There are several reasons.

Let's consider physical handicaps first. A physical impairment such as blindness, deafness, loss of a limb, disfiguration or debilitating disease often causes an individual to develop strength in another area. This requires unusual effort and unwavering persistence. It demands concentration and determination. It requires the best of what one has inside to overcome a weakness outside.

Financial setbacks challenge not only our accounting skills, they often necessitate patience and the ability to plan long-range and to tighten the belt immediately. Money problems often drive us to seek counsel from others. This particular characteristic is common to most serious problems and is probably the most beneficial aspect of trouble. As we begin talking to other people, several things become clear: We are not alone in our troubles, other people can understand what we face, and our problems do have solutions.

With this kind of knowledge, we are then better able to dig in, work hard, and overcome our difficulties. What is the end result? Triumph, exhilaration and a tremendous boost to our self-confidence.

Should we give thanks for our problems? Absolutely. It is only through struggle that we become stronger and surer of our capabilities. Heat and pressure are the great forgers of purity and strength. Give thanks when your capabilities are challenged, for such times present the best opportunities for growth.

Human Fireflies

One of my all-time favorite things about summer is watching fireflies. They float silently, lighting up the evening dusk with their cheerful twinkling. Such magical creatures they are! How do they light up? How many times can one firefly light in an evening, in a lifetime? Why do they only appear for a few short weeks during the summer?

In doing some quick research, I learned that glowing fireflies are typically not found west of Kansas. They are generally found in warm, humid areas of the world—like summertime in Wisconsin!

Their flashing behavior is primarily designed to find mates. During a certain time of night males fly about flashing their species-specific flash pattern. Females of the same species tend to be perched on vegetation, usually near the ground, and if a flashing male catches her fancy, she will respond at a fixed time delay after the male's last flash. A short flash dialogue may ensue between the male and female as he locates her position.

Fireflies invariably make me think about people. Do you know a human firefly? Someone who sparkles with positive energy, lights up a room, and brings smiles to the faces of those who see her? I am fortunate to know several. Their smiles are like a firefly's flash.

But where the firefly flashes solely to find a mate, human fireflies can inspire and encourage others to show their brilliance as well. In this case, they become fire-lighters.

A fire-lighter is the sort of person who enjoys her life and appreciates the gifts of others. She is keenly aware of special energy reflected in someone's eyes or smile or manner and when she detects a spark, she fans it. A fire-lighter encourages lively thinking and timely action. She lends support and enthusiasm to others by engaging in thoughtful, sometimes spirited, discussion and constructive feedback. She is genuinely interested in the thoughts and ideas of others; she recognizes many opportunities to advance her own knowledge as well. A fire-lighter's facial expressions tend to be lively and she talks eyeball to eyeball.

A fire-fighter, on the other hand, is the proverbial wet blanket. This woman kills new ideas and projects by pointing out, with great sensibility, why the new suggestions won't work. A naysayer of the highest order, she scorns enthusiasm as immature or irrational. She prefers impersonality, avoids direct eye contact during conversation, and displays an attitude of studied sophistication. Think of your disapproving Aunt Gertrude.

Enthusiasm is anathema to the fire-fighter who likes to keep things orderly and subdued. The enthusiast is stereotyped in the fire-fighter's mind as the child be-bopping around—smiling, waving, and talking a lot about very little that makes sense.

Enthusiasm, however, can be much more subtle. It manifests itself in unusual stamina, focused energy and sharp, multidimensional thinking that produces great new ideas. Zeal is another word that is normally viewed askance because of its unfortunate connotation of religious fervor. A zealot is too eager, too passionate, too one-dimensional in her thinking, too enthusiastic—a fanatic.

And yet, to fireflies and fire-lighters, enthusiasm and zeal are comfortable words. They lie at the heart of great effort in any walk of life. They need not be obnoxiously visible; indeed they are sometimes better held as private motivators. But fire-lighters see these tendencies working within others and they encourage the action. They recognize potential and purposely seek to develop it. Fire-fighters recognize enthusiasm and zeal, too. They work hard to squelch such inclinations before they get out of control.

You can recognize both types by the way they show up. Fire-lighters have a presence and luminescence about them; they look happy, engaged, and eager to meet you. Fire-fighters, on the other hand, look dull, disinterested; they make you want to take their pulse. They make you want to find something else to do that does not include them.

As a fire-lighter, you can share your light and help make things happen. As a fire-fighter, you may have a hand in quelling silly notions—and potentially great ones as well. Which vocation will you choose?

Love Your Life

February is the month of hearts and flowers, candlelight and romance. For people lucky enough to be in love, that is. For people who are alone or in a less than satisfying relationship, February is just another cold winter month full of snow and ice and survival challenges. Groundhog Day is an apt marker.

But even for people in love, Valentine's Day feels less exuberant this year because there is so much to worry about.

What if you decided to stop worrying? What if, when you took time to consider what's truly important, you decided the economy didn't matter? What if you realized you had enough each day to feel comfortable, with hope enough to build a better future? Stop for a moment and take stock of your life. You may find that you have everything you need to get through this day with some— maybe a lot— left over for tomorrow.

Here's good news: You can love your life! No matter its current condition, you have the capacity to make it different. You get to choose who you want to be, what you want to do, and how you want to live.

Many women dispute this truth. They point to spouses or partners or friends or families who have different ideas and who impose those ideas with the implication that if a woman doesn't play by their rules they will not be loved.

But those others are simply telling you how they see life. They have formed habits of thinking and doing that comprise the rules. Where is the book that says you must conform? Where did the notion of self-denial creep into the definition of successful relationships? What unhappy woman makes others happy? It doesn't make sense.

Still, the fear of rejection paralyzes many women and robs them of the joy that arrives fresh each morning with the rising of the sun. Did you notice the sunrise this morning? Did you feel the warmth inside the early morning silence?

If you're like many women, you simply don't have time for such things. There's too much on your mind, too many kids to point in the right direction, too many noisy details of life that crowd out the quiet. Too bad.

I'd like to challenge today's callow notions of happiness and encourage you to dig deeper. Take time—make time!—to ponder the goodness you are surrounded by each day. Appreciation is a wonderful antidote to stress. It is a habit you can cultivate.

Think of the things you collect and display in your living space. Photos, mementoes, ribbons, ticket stubs, trophies, bits of fabric and color, special songs. As collections grow, appreciation can subside. Artifacts blend into the backgrounds of our lives and we forget the importance of each item.

To rejuvenate joy and appreciation – to truly love your life – take time each week to stop and appreciate a favorite picture, statue, or trinket that represents a loving connection. Remember who gave it to you or the special place you found it. Close your eyes and allow a quiet moment to savor the memory.

Take note of the wonders of your life. What has made a difference to you? Who has touched you in a memorable way? What dreams do you have?

You may want to start a Goodness Journal. At the end of each day, note one thing that made you think, "that's good." It may be something you saw, someone you met, something you ate or drank. When you keep track of goodness, you may be amazed at how often you encounter it!

Loving your life is a matter of choice, not circumstance. Yes, yes, you know this. But an intellectual understanding is a far cry from an emotional embracing of this truth. Only you can decide that your life is right, just as it is.

As we celebrate Valentine's Day, let's note the good things in our lives and do more of them. Let's fall in love with who we are, the times we live in, and the stories our lives will ultimately tell. To accept anything less is to belie the fabulous women we are!

Mama Said There'd Be Days Like This!

We've all had them. The days you hit the snooze button and wish you could forget about getting up. The days you think about the problems and obnoxious people waiting for you at work and figure you'd rather have typhoid fever. The days it feels like nothing good will happen so your best bet is to stay out of harm's way by staying home.

Mama said there'd be days like this! If your mama never got around to warning you about them, there's a song by the Shirelles that lets you know she should have. And if you, Mama, haven't said to your kids they can expect days like this, it's time you did.

Difficult days are a part of everyone's life. Difficult people at work are, too. Some things you can count on, whether you'd like to or not.

What you need to know – whether mama said it or not - about dealing with days like this is that the key to maintaining a strong and happy perspective on them starts with you. Your attitude, focus, and determination will get you through "days like this."

So what is the attitude? I'd recommend acceptance and curiosity. When you accept that these days are going to be challenging, maybe supremely annoying, you give yourself permission to not respond. It's like waking up to a big snowfall after Spring has officially arrived. You can't do anything about it, but you don't need to invest a lot of emotional energy in dealing with it, either.

Curiosity is a little trickier. When you're ticked off, it's hard to conjure up curiosity. But if you can figuratively scratch your head and wonder what might come of a potential catfight if you could change your interaction with a testy co-worker, the outcome might make your day. That's one example. Another might be anticipating a challenging question in a meeting and being curious about the question rather than defensive about the challenge.

Focus is about knowing what you want to achieve or experience during the course of the day. When you start out with a picture of what you want to have happen in your mind, you will be more likely to experience it or something close to it than if you started the day with a blank slate and a crabby attitude.

We all have an enormous amount of noise and distraction to deal with day to day. When you can focus on what is important to you in achieving the day's goals and your longer term objectives, you get better at tuning out the noise and ignoring the distractions.

Determination is probably the most difficult quality to muster when you're feeling like you'd rather stay home on the porch than head out into a confrontational world. In order to feel determined, you must have a positive goal in mind; one that makes you feel strong and proud of yourself as you imagine attaining it. The picture of a successful you and the good feelings you have because of it are what drive determination.

Determination is dependent on focus. If you don't know where you're going, any road will take you there. Any time frame will, too. And any outcome is potentially okay.

When Mama said there'd be days like this, she was thinking of exceptions to your motivated and excited journey into the future. Consider difficult days to be just that. Exceptions. With the proper mindset, they can be valuable reality checks. They offer opportunities to stop for a moment to think about where you are going, why you want to go there, and what you are choosing along the way.

"Days like this" are gifts! Embrace their questions and listen carefully to your answers. "Days like this" lead to days of purposeful action, which reward us with satisfaction and joy. Mama said there'd be days like this, but she may have forgotten to tell you how lucky you are to have them.

Nature's Fury and Brilliance

*I*t was a rare winter storm. Silent mists froze in incremental layers, weighing down then breaking trees and power lines, making traffic look like Bambi on ice, skittering helter skelter, and sending all under cover as darkness closed the curtain on a damaging weather play.

And then, brilliance. The extravaganza put on by Mother Nature the next day was a continuous showing of spectacular 'art,' free of charge. Every tree and shrub wore strings of diamonds that swayed seductively and glittered in dazzling sunshine, creating a fairyland of enchantment that I, for one, had never seen before.

Did you miss it? Did its beauty escape you? Were you preoccupied by cutting away dead tree limbs and chopping ice off of sidewalks and driveways? If so, I am sorry for you. Yes, the amazing beauty was marred by wide spread damage. Inconvenience, loss of property, and fear are not harbingers of appreciation. Broken trees and sawed off branches remind us that we sometimes pay a dear price at the hand of nature. But she evened the score with a display of beauty so rare that it gave an awesome perspective to the preceding trouble.

The balance is a delicate one, certainly, and you may not agree that the visual spectacle was worth the physical discomfort. But nature, through this experience, provides us with a valuable lesson. There is an ebb and flow to life, a balance of cruelty and beauty, of good and bad. We don't always understand it; at times we can only accept it.

Our challenge is to learn to see past the bad to the good; to understand that beyond the darkness lies the dawn; and to be able to clear our minds of the harshness in order to appreciate the awe-inspiring beauty that follows.

Nowhere Man

Meet Stanley. Stanley is the genius in his company this year. Stanley spearheaded the development of a new product line that became the success of the century and now he's a new product consultant. Stanley always knows just the right thing to say in every situation. Stanley is smart, educated at the best schools by the best professors. Stanley is handsome. Stanley is rich. Stanley is an outstanding father, a model husband, and the best Little League coach in town. Stanley loves to go bowling with the guys, drink beer and shoot pool. He lends money to his friends, goes to church every Sunday and never criticizes people with different opinions. What a guy, that Stanley.

But Stanley is unhappy. He has no real friends, no close friends. Stanley tries to be all things to all people and because of that, nobody knows exactly who Stanley is. Stanley is a generic in his own mind. He fits in anywhere because he doesn't have any private label thoughts or ideas. Before he speaks or acts in any given situation, his barometer is checking out the atmospheric pressure. And for Stanley, the pressure is always on. He is truly a master at being everybody's main man… and a nowhere man.

Stanley doesn't know who Stanley is. He's deathly afraid of being pinned down to what he thinks. Or of getting into a mixed group where he'll be forced to sit on the fence. Or of making a decision without direct input from others.

Poor Stanley is an enigma. Because nobody has a handle on who he is, nobody really cares about him. Some folks envy him; some think he's a pretty cool guy; most folks don't think about him one way or another. No one chooses Stanley to be a best friend. Stanley is confused. What Stanley does not know is this:

> *The most agreeable of all companions is a simple, frank man, without any high pretensions to an oppressive greatness; one who loves life and understands the use of it; obliging, alike at all hours; above all, of a golden temper and steadfast as an anchor. For such a one we gladly exchange the great genius, the most brilliant wit, the profoundest thinker.*
> —Gotthold Ephraim Lessing

Players, not Quitters

*I*magine life as a card game. Gathered around the table are people we all know: Mr. Disgruntled, who chews a cigar and grunts through his smoke clouds; Mr. Nervous, whose gaze flicks back and forth between the players and his cards; Mr. Cool, who has no expression and no apparent concern for the outcome of the game. He is all cool, calm control.

Then there is Mr. Big Bet, who is as free with his money as he is with this mouth, and his counterpart, Mr. Timid, who is afraid to stake a bet and afraid to play his cards. He winds up sitting the fence and reacting to everyone else. Mr. Complaint, by far the most vocal, always has a reason for losing. He gets rotten cards, has a run of bad luck, or decides the game is stupid or rigged.

Out of all these different characters, Mr. Complaint is the guy who lives to some extent in all of us. When our card game isn't going well, we like to think it's the dealer's fault, fate's fault or the stupid game's fault. Unfortunately, those excuses aren't worth much.

Got rotten cards? You can do one of two things: trade them in, hoping to get better ones, or play them the best you can and wait for a better hand. The dealer simply deals the cards. There is no fault in that.

Had a run of bad luck? That's hardly fate's fault. Bad luck happens. There is no explaining it and sometimes there is no averting it. It's a fact of life. Fortunately, bad luck runs in streaks interspersed with good luck. If you can learn to endure streaks of bad luck, you not only beat them, but you develop patience and persistence to boot.

The game is stupid? Well, some people do feel that way and tragically opt out. They throw in their cards, cave in to bad luck, cash in their chips. It is the quitter's way, the easy way out.

Most of us, however, stick with the game. Many of us learn to see life as a challenge, an invitation to use our wits and our guts, instead of as a stupid game. We learn to be players instead of quitters. And here is the best news: If we stick with it long enough and learn the subtleties of the game, we can come out real winners in life.

Self-Confidence is for Everyone

*There is a kind of greatness which does not depend upon
fortune; it is a certain manner that distinguishes us, and
which seems to destine us for great things; it is the value we
insensibly set upon ourselves; it is by this quality that we gain
the deference of others, and it is this which commonly raises
us more above them than birth, rank, or even merit itself.*
—La Rochefoucauld

*T*he quality so highly praised above is self-confidence.
Self-confidence is not inherited, it is not learned in higher
education courses; it is not bestowed upon us by beneficent
others, nor is it garnered as an automatic by-product of living. This we
know all too well!

Self-confidence is forged under fire by taking a shot at the things
which frighten us most. Only by challenging ourselves to confront life's
difficulties do we develop the capabilities that ultimately ripen into self-
confidence. It is not an entirely private thing; it is nurtured by the
commendations of those around us. True self-confidence is not,
however, destroyed by the criticism or disapproval of others.

At its finest, self-confidence becomes a solid, calm self-trust at the
core of our being which allows us to present ourselves with assurance

and dignity no matter what challenge we encounter. Self-confidence takes us to places where a lack of formal education or training might forbid us to go.

Self-confidence allows us to shake another's hand in an attitude of respect and appreciation when we might otherwise be intimidated by status or stature. Self-confidence allows us to open doors, speak thoughts, and welcome opposition with fearlessness and poise. Indeed, with curiosity.

Self-confidence, with all its many benefits, allows us to open up fully to life; to embrace challenge; to acknowledge failure and learn from it; to experiment with the possibilities before us courageously, hopefully, happily.

Self-confidence is available to all. But you have to step into life in order to find it, hone it, and appreciate its power.

Sweet Success

*H*ave you ever thought of success in terms of making someone else's life easier? It's not likely that you have. Society today teaches us to think of success in terms of money, fame, a big house, prestigious car, smart kids, rich friends, invitations to big events and sundry other things. The focus is on ourselves; the emphasis on acquisition.

Could making life easier for someone else work as a definition of success? Let's test the idea in familiar situations like family, schools and work.

In a family setting, what is a successful parent? Someone who raises a child to be attentive, respectful, cheerful, intelligent and sensitive to the needs of others. Right?

What about the parent who makes life easier for a child by listening attentively, discussing youthful problems carefully, offering alternatives without insisting that a particular one be followed, and viewing mistakes as lessons in life rather than shameful failures?

Notice that making life easier for a child does not include chauffeuring him around his paper route, cleaning his room, providing special comforts and the like. Growing up is hard and accepting responsibility even harder. The successful parent does not eliminate these struggles, he or she makes it easier for a child to talk about them and seek help when necessary.

Is success at school defined as superior grades by students and brilliant instruction by teachers? Or could it mean students who listen for the knowledge they want to gain and teachers who make lessons relevant and interesting to the people they are directing? There's no doubt that students can make teachers' jobs easier and vice versa.

Success at work generally means a big title, a big salary and the corner office with a big view, right? Why not think of your job in terms of making life easier for people around you and above you? The successful worker could be defined as one who does a job profession-ally, efficiently, with good humor and in such a way as to allow others to do their jobs well.

It looks from this perspective like success is, as many things in life are, contingent on attitude. If you are out to get, you may succeed and you many not. If you are out to give, you can't help but win.

Why not try today to make life easier for someone close to you? You may not make the annals of history, but you can make a difference to someone you know. The taste of success is sweet; the joy of helping another, indescribable.

The Age of the Babbling Brook

*I*t's a pleasant sound, the gurgling and bubbling that a shallow stream creates as it trips over stones and sticks and other objects in its pathway. Stopping to appreciate it, one can be refreshed in just a few moments or linger longer, becoming mesmerized by the sound.

Our social surroundings have become a lot like these shallow streams. Endless gurgling and bubbling—babbling—that tends not to refresh but rather wear us down over time. The innumerable talking heads on TV, the shallow but urgent utterances of reality TV show characters, the constant buzzing of technology hovers nearby. To babble means to prattle, stammer, make incoherent sounds; to talk foolishly or too much.

I have noticed an emerging sentiment over the past eight or nine months with regard to this phenomenon. More and more women are telling me that they long for a conversation that has some depth, some substance, some meaning. They are tired of the endless chatter that surrounds them and they find it increasingly difficult to pay attention.

At the same time, some of these women admit that they are much more vocal than they have been in the past. They feel that in order to be heard they must talk more frequently and at a higher volume. Unfortunately, as women's voices get louder, they tend to rise in pitch as well. This can begin to sound like hysteria. Whether or not a woman starts out feeling emotional, she may become so if she doesn't believe her voice is valued.

She may begin to repeat herself. She may begin to feel disrespected. She may become angry or resentful of others who seem to get more attention. Sometimes this frustration is summarized as a problem of the "old boys network" or the "glass ceiling."

The fact is that we live in the Age of the Babbling Brook. Currently there are more than 20,000 media outlets including traditional radio, TV and print publications as well as cable and Internet services.

A quick glance at growth in the cable business shows that in 1952, this new industry included 70 cable systems serving 14,000 subscribers. By the end of the 1980s, satellite technology had expanded service to 53 million households. A decade later, 65 million households had access to at least 54 channels.

Broadband networks now provide multi-channel video, two-way voice, high-speed Internet and high definition and advanced digital video services on a single line into a home. This has allowed more people in more places (urban, suburban, and rural) more choices in information, communication, and entertainment services.

Add to this recent estimates of LinkedIn and FaceBook subscriptions totaling more than 250 million subscribers in countries circling the globe.

That's a lot of noise and a lot of choices to process.

It's no wonder people are having a hard time finding meaning in conversation. If you are feeling similarly overwhelmed and dissatisfied, there are some simple things you can do. Simple, but not easy.

First, recognize your own patterns of information consumption and media usage. How often are you online or in front of a TV or movie screen? What information do you purposely seek? What types of images or information get you sidetracked? How much time do you spend with telecommunications networks vs. human interaction?

Second, recognize that your voice competes with this vast ocean of noise. When you speak, make your words meaningful. When you write, get to the point. When you seek answers, be specific with your questions. And when you want to learn, quiet your mind to truly listen.

There is tremendous discipline involved in living on purpose. This is not new, for there have always been distractions. However, there probably has never been an age that has felt so universally and globally competitive.

Take time to listen to yourself and sort through your goals and dreams. Decide where you want to go. Seek credible guidance and make your way with determination and joy. In an age of babble, you can stand out as the still water that runs deep. You'll discover greater satisfaction and maybe make a meaningful new connection or two.

The Downside of Helping Too Much

ince the dawn of time, parents have wanted a better life for their children. Our country has a rich history of people who struggled and sacrificed to create opportunity for themselves and their families. Hard work, belief in just rewards, and sheer determination brought success to many. And always, they dreamed of easier times and a better life for their children.

Certainly we celebrate progress and the fact that life is far easier today than it was generations ago is a hallmark of success. But the pendulum has swung too far.

We hear too much these days about trophy kids and helicopter parents; kids who have never wanted for anything and the doting parents who make sure they never will. This makes me wonder when the notion of a better life changed from meaning one of more opportunity and hard work to one of no worries, no work, and no disappointments.

There is irony in this progress. In wanting to protect loved ones from all harm and worry, we end up creating deeper vulnerability.

Think about how we learn. To ride a bike, we have to learn not only the concept, but the feeling of balance. A critical part of this learning is experiencing what unbalance feels like. We have to tip over! In tipping over, we often scrape a knee or an elbow. We experience pain. It is not debilitating!

Unless, of course, a parent freaks out and runs to the rescue. Then we learn that maybe we don't have the right internal calibrator for pain. Maybe it was far worse than we thought. Given Mom or Dad's response, surely this must be so.

So next time we tip over for whatever reason, we look for a freaked out parent, exaggerate the experience, oversell the pain, and get the attention we expect when something unfortunate happens.

Play this out over tender developmental years and it's no surprise that coping skills fade. Without coping skills, people don't know what to do when difficulties arise. Scared people wait, like children, for someone to come to their rescue. The louder they wail, the faster they expect help will arrive.

But that's not how the world works.

Here's what happens to people who are over-cared for or micro-managed:

 ◆ They do not learn to recognize – or solve—problems.

 ◆ They learn that someone, somewhere will take care of everything that makes them uncomfortable.

 ◆ As they wait, they become more vulnerable.

 ◆ They do not learn their own capacity.

 ◆ They are robbed of the satisfaction that comes from determined effort to surmount a challenge.

- They lose the chance to feel the pride and joy of realizing success at their own hands.

- They never develop an understanding of their own strength, resourcefulness, and ability to choose.

As for the caretakers who go overboard:

- They are constantly on guard against real and imagined threats.

- They are never thanked for their efforts because the ones they protect never learn to see danger.

- There is no end to the resources they must invest, even when they are ready to stop helping so much.

- There is no way to feel proud of what they have taught, for their protégés never learn to be independent.

- In time, they grow weary of the timidity and whining of the very ones they have made dependent.

Here's a sad truth: When we take care of every potential difficulty for a child or subordinate, we teach dependence and, whether we realize it or not, we destroy confidence. Not only that, we wear ourselves out in the process!

Why would anyone choose this behavior? Perhaps we get so caught up in wanting to 'make life better' that we cannot see these effects. Perhaps we do not know any alternative. It is time to teach a better way!

Parents, practice letting go in small ways while your children are growing up. Stay close to help heal bruises and discover lessons, but don't try to prevent all bumps.

Bosses, give assignments and let people do them. Do not peer over their shoulders to inspect their every move. Stay accessible to answer questions and provide guidance when it is requested. Recognize progress and celebrate growth. You are instilling strength and confidence, two characteristics that support a better life for all.

The Lesson of the Sleeping Bag

*I*f you are like most people, you try to solve your problems your way—alone. There are two common reasons for this: 1) you wish to project a strong image (I don't need help), and 2) you don't feel right about burdening others with your troubles. Unfortunately, you may fail to realize how silly it is to put off seeking help.

Imagine that you are sleeping in a sleeping bag that is zipped all the way up. As problems cross your mind during the night, you burrow deeper and deeper into the sleeping bag. Soon you get to the bottom and begin tossing and turning.

By morning you have flip-flopped and are now upside down in the sleeping bag, struggling to find the opening. As you punch and flail trying to get out, you become not only further entangled, but angry as well. Fear sneaks in, too, as you wonder how you'll ever get out of the thing.

To someone standing on the outside, the scene is quite hilarious. This person sees the situation clearly. He can see the solution to your problem (the zipper) and would have little difficulty in releasing you from your struggles. He would, of course, first have to convince you that he could indeed help you out. And you would have to trust him.

The analogy applies to your life. Are you struggling now with a problem that seems insurmountable? Do you feel caught—trapped without any idea about where to go for help? Are you punching and flailing at the wrong end of life's sleeping bag?

If so, still your struggles long enough to holler for help. There is someone out there with a better perspective. Very likely, there is someone who was once trapped, just like you, at the wrong end of a sleeping bag. Ask that someone to open the zipper.

You might feel embarrassed at first when you crawl out, disheveled from the experience. You can, however, square your shoulders, stand up straight, and emerge from your tussle with dignity. You have struggled and triumphed. And you have been big enough to ask someone for help.

Sometimes we encounter problems that seem to have no solutions. Instead of giving up and suffocating at the wrong end of a sleeping bag, you can cut your misery considerably by learning to go to someone who understands and cares about your troubles.

The Magic Three

How have you been feeling lately? Energetic, enthusiastic, fit, mentally sharp and happy? Or are you down in the dumps, literally? Do you have a dumpy body, a dumpy job, dumpy friends? Don't blame it on the weather; you have a dumpy attitude.

This down-in-the-dumps syndrome gets everyone at one time or another. Generally, it's no cause for worry. But sometimes…

You find an ailment in your body that didn't used to be there. You have a recurring stiff neck, sore knee, or aching back. You have trouble with an upset stomach. Your eyes hurt. You get headaches. You can't seem to fall asleep and when you do, it is only for brief periods. Your diet doesn't work the way it used to and you are convinced that you are losing your hair.

Over time, these little frets can grow into big concerns and you may consult a doctor. Psychosomatic, he pronounces. All your diagnostic tests run clean. Now what?

Now you have several choices. You can forget your ailments and get on with life. You can consult another physician. You can nurture your hurts as little excuses to live less than fully. Sometimes it makes sense to get a second professional opinion. This is especially true if the ailment interferes with your regular activities. Most often, however, if you are in good physical condition generally, you are better off involving yourself in other things that will take your mind off your aches and pains. After a few weeks, you may be surprised to notice that they have disappeared.

How are you feeling? If you feel good, great. Share your good fortune with others. If not, here's a tip from a simpler time. If you need a physician, employ these three: a cheerful mind, rest, and a temperate diet.

The Story in a Smile

A smile is a wonderful thing. It is a physical expression of what is happening in someone's head. Types of smiles are as limitless as types of personality and every bit as interesting.

Look, for instance, at the subtleties of the Mona Lisa or the wrinkled wisdom of Red Skelton. Contrast the tender smile of a mother with the enchanted smile of a child on Christmas morning. Picture the demonical grin of the Joker or the cynical smirk of Clint Eastwood. Each one is a unique expression that masks or reveals the feelings within the individual.

There are so many smiles, I bet we could construct a smile alphabet of different types we encounter. For instance, there is an amused smile, a bewildered smile, a candid smile, and a defensive smile. A smile can be effusive, forthright, gorgeous, hesitant, inimical, joyful, or knowing. I have seen smiles that are lazy, meaningful, non-descript, open, pensive, questioning and radiant. Sunny, timid, understanding, vain, wistful, xenophobic (look it up), yearning, and zany might all describe smiles you have seen.

Watch people smile. Pay special attention to the people you talk to. Learn to read expressions, to see not only the tensing or relaxing of facial muscles, but the glimmering or dullness of the eyes. You'll discover much more about people than they might tell you in words.

Watching people smile has other benefits, too. It is a good way to take your mind off yourself. By concentrating on another, it is possible to overcome self-consciousness and timidity. You may find you have the gift of making others smile. And if you can make someone smile from way down within—a smile that shines in the eyes as well as on the face—you will have made a friend.

We Think We're Something

S ome time ago, I saw a TV movie in which a dying father told his son, "We're born with nothing, we end up with nothing, but in between, we think we're something."

What a profound statement. The more I thought about it, the more intriguing its message became. It occurred to me that this statement was a beautiful illustration of the difference between a positive and a negative outlook.

The individual with a negative attitude will look at the statement and say, "If we're born with nothing and end up with nothing, why bother trying to be anything in between? What difference does it make?" Taken from this perspective, indeed what difference does life make? The end result of such thinking is often deep depression and despair.

Looking at the statement from another, more positive viewpoint, we can see that because we start with nothing and end up with nothing, anything we accomplish in between is fantastic. To make something from nothing is to create. But we must realize that we had more than nothing to begin with.

Each of us was born with incredible potential. And we have a lifetime to develop this potential into something truly outstanding.

Problems arise, though, when we try to define "something." Does being something mean becoming important in the sense of accumulating wealth or fame? Or could it simply mean living a decent, thoughtful life? The matter—and the definition—is personal and relative.

Beneath the surface of this statement we find two gentle reminders.

First, maintain a sense of humor. It is a tremendous aid in keeping things in perspective.

Second, learn and understand the meaning of humility. After all, even the greatest accomplishments are fleeting.

We are born with nothing, we end up with nothing, but in between we think we're something. Use your time in between to be something, whatever you conceive "something" to be. Although you will not live forever, the impressions you leave can last a long, long time.

What Do You Expect?

D o you have more to offer than anyone realizes? Many women do. The question I wonder about is why? Why do you have more to offer and why doesn't anyone realize it?

There are a few quick answers. You are so busy taking care of everyday things there is no time left for extra offerings. You are too tired to push yourself beyond the normal routine. There is no reward for offering more, especially if no one is looking for it.

That last answer tells a big story about what you expect from life, your work, or relationships. If you give primarily to get, your energy is likely to be used up fairly quickly. But if you give because you enjoy the feeling of challenging yourself and finding ways to contribute, your energy becomes self-renewing.

Let's look at Louise, who does what is expected of her and little else, and Shayna, who is like a perpetual motion machine, always looking for something interesting to do.

Louise can often be heard at work saying, "That's not my job." She refuses to work past her company's official closing time and would never think about taking work home at night or on weekends. She believes that the company would take everything she has to give and still want more, while paying her the least amount of money they can get away with.

Louise feels the same way about her husband and kids. They would run her ragged then run over the top of her if she let them. They are always asking for more, but when she needs something, they are unavailable. She believes that if she had a stroke and died, they would plop her in a grave on their way to finding their next servant.

Louise is very pragmatic about all this. She is not angry or resentful because she has drawn firm boundaries around herself. She is not going to allow anyone to take advantage of her. She does admit, however, that she is almost always tired. She admits that she could be giving more—a lot more—if anyone would appreciate what she already gives.

Then there's Shayna. She is always looking for new and interesting people, places, and things to learn about and get connected to. Her life is full—sometimes too full—but she is rarely tired. She thrives on activity and is refreshed by her interactions with others. At work, Shayna delivers what she promises. She is quick to ask for help when she needs it and keen to learn from her colleagues.

Interestingly, Shayna does not seem to care about who notices her or appreciates what she does. When people ask her for things she is not able or willing to give them, she says no with a smile. Then she goes about her day. You never get the sense that Shayna is measuring her life in terms of giving and getting; she is too busy enjoying herself. Asked whether she might have more to give, she says, "probably, but only if there were more hours in the day."

This is more than a story of different personalities. It is a demonstration of the way expectations can make you sick or keep you healthy. Louise expects to be taken advantage of so she is continually watching others, weighing their words and judging their intentions. Her energy is taken up in this constant assessment and she has little time to simply be herself.

Shayna expects to reap benefits after she has sown effort. She takes responsibility for her happiness and allows others to do the same. She begrudges no one his or her successes, nor does she feel anyone owes her a hand in creating hers. Because she accepts life as it is, she is free of the emotional burden of wishing it were different.

If you feel you have more to give, you have several choices. You can develop the gifts you have or tap into that something more to see what it is. You can shrug your shoulders and ignore the feeling. You can forget about who might be watching or what that something more might be worth. You can decide to live your best life just because you can.

What's Next?

*H*ave you ever reached a point in your life where you look around yourself and think: I've come this far and done pretty well, but I have an urge inside that makes me want to do more?

Perhaps you've experienced a different, darker, version of this feeling that makes you think you're not as far along as you should be at this stage of your life. If so, you're not alone. And you're not weird. The "What's Next?" question arises for everyone at some point.

For some women, these life assessments can trigger mild to moderate depression, especially when they compare themselves to others they consider more successful.

Here's a question: Why do we always look up and judge ourselves deficient instead of looking all around and feeling grateful for where we are? A hyper-competitive world and relentless media attention on beauty, money, and fame may have a lot to do with it!

But so does our thinking. We create a lifeline in our mind's eye and we mark, sometimes unconsciously, the milestones we feel we should reach by certain ages. We should be promoted by this age. We should be in a committed relationship, have a house, family, fantastic car, diamonds on our right hand and maybe a vacation home in some island destination according to a specific and aggressive timetable.

These benchmarks of success have ratcheted up dramatically over the years. It used to be that if you earned $1,000 for every year you are old, you were doing very well. Can you imagine earning only $35,000 a year if you're 35 years old? LOSER!

Changing times and changing fortunes aside, what's a woman to do when she comes face to face with What's Next?

By all means, listen to the inner voice that's saying you want to do and be more. Spend some time imagining what that might be. Imagine, too, who might be willing to support or help you create what's next. But don't let it make you crazy. And please don't lose the value and joy of today because you're clouded over emotionally about what might or might not be tomorrow.

Life goes by quickly, whether it feels that way or not sometimes. And it plays out in chapters, not in a seamless or inevitable series of advances.

Think about your favorite novel or movie. There are probably moments of sunshine and happiness that inspire you. There are probably also moments of great darkness, distress, and near despair that make you wonder if your favorite character will prevail.

Without being overly dramatic, that storyline is true for each of us. We have periods of life when things click. Kids do well in school, our partners look good and do things to make us happy; even pets behave. And then there are times when we are convinced that the devil has taken control of our lives turning our kids, co-workers, lovers and friends into exploiters and greedy one-eyed monsters.

You'll notice that great literature includes, but does not settle into, positive or negative chapters. They blend dark and light to create powerful stories of compassion, heroism, and accomplishment. Isn't that true for your life as well?

If you examine it, I think you will find that it is. But we get stuck in the negative chapters, fearing that the rest of our lives will be dark. We gloss over the positive ones as being lucky and not likely to recur.

Take some time to consider your life so far. Dream about what you would like it to be before it's over. You are the director of your life's story. There are things you can choose and admittedly, things you'll end up enduring. But if you're thoughtful and skillful, you can blend them into a true story that is charming, challenging, inspirational, and worthy of your investment of time, thought, energy, love, and endurance.

What's Next? It's yours to choose! Make it meaningful to you because then it may be a gift of inspiration to another.

You Do Not Need a Bailout

*H*onestly, you don't. If you worry about the economy, your job, your finances—your future—you are not alone. But worry robs you of important energy you need to move forward. So does the idea that you need a bailout to survive. You don't! What you need is 1) a thorough and objective review of your situation, 2) a plan for moving forward, and 3) belief in yourself and a decision to work patiently day to day to improve.

Step One: Review your situation
Things have changed dramatically over the past six months. Truth is, "things" change every day for good or ill. You don't notice this incremental change because you're busy living your life. But all of a sudden someone looks old. Your finances have dwindled. Your stability feels shaken.

Before you can decide what you want to do about your current situation, you have to understand what it truly looks like. Make an inventory of your assets as they are valued today. Don't just count money and stuff; think about your friendships, family relationships, and business associations. Forget about what you've lost—it's history. Staying stuck in anger or depression will only diminish your ability to move forward and rebuild.

Step Two: Make a plan

With a current inventory in hand, think about what you want to keep and what you're ready to part with. e-Bay, garage sales, the classifieds, word-of-mouth advertising, even the barter system are ways to clear out unwanted materials. Many non-profit agencies would be glad to have your discards.

Reflect on your relationships. Are there some that wear you down? Are there others that make you feel strong and hopeful? Spend your time wisely.

Get your financial house in order. Whether you work with a financial planner or on your own, set goals for paying off bills, boosting savings, and rebuilding your financial foundation. This will not be an easy task, nor will your decisions suddenly create easier circumstances. But when you think through your options and create a plan aimed at restoration, your stress will subside.

Step Three: Believe in yourself.

Determine to be patient and persistent. Although your losses may feel sudden and catastrophic, they are neither. With consistent effort and a confident mindset, you will restore yourself.

If you need help, ask for it! You may feel embarrassed or shamed by your current situation, but don't let that stop you from reaching out. People are still interested in helping one another.

The most important thing you can do during a time of acute challenge is to believe in yourself and focus on your health. Get some exercise. Eat good food. Lay off the booze and junk food. Turn off the lights and get some sleep.

Read uplifting articles, books, and magazines. Wean yourself from the daily barrage of doom and gloom; it only wears down your optimism and resolve.

Ralph Waldo Emerson was an American essayist, philosopher and poet who lived in the 1800s. He traveled widely, studied broadly, and networked with great thinkers of his day. His essay, Self Reliance, offers bold advice that makes sense even today. Here are a few (edited) tidbits to ponder:

Trust thyself. Accept the place the divine providence has found for you, the society of your contemporaries, the connection of events.

Whoso would be a man must be a nonconformist.

What I must do is all that concerns me, not what the people think. This rule may serve for the whole distinction between greatness and meanness. It is the harder, because you will always find those who think they know what is your duty better than you know it.

Do your work, and I shall know you. Do your work, and you shall reinforce yourself.

This sage advice was difficult to follow in Emerson's day. It may be even more difficult in our age of distraction. But if you take the time to examine your life, find ways to improve it, and patiently go about your work, you will be a powerful and happy woman of substance.

You? Intelligent? Yes!

ifferent people have different ideas about intelligence. Scientists like to group people by IQ numbers. Others look at things like speed of comprehension, aptitude for numbers or other specialized skills, glibness, broadness of experience, or insight into human behavior for indications of intelligence.

Lots of people assume that the (controlled) erratic or bizarre among us are simply over-endowed with intelligence and sensitivity and therefore are unable to relate to the hardheadedness of the real world.

Now, I am certainly no scientist or theoretician, but it seems to me that the most intelligent people are those who have the ability to function happily and effectively in their particular surroundings. As simple and innocent as this sounds, it entails a complex interaction with many elements. For example, all of us live with time pressures, performance expectations, and challenges to our physical, mental and emotional well-being.

I may not have a lofty IQ, but I understand very clearly the problems that jump out at me every day. And, generally speaking, I handle most of them reasonably well. I can predict with a measure of accuracy the results of my actions. I know facts and figures about a fair number of subjects, and I can pick up on the behavior of others pretty well. Does this make me an intelligent person? Perhaps. But how smart am I when I scream at a nine-year old child because I've had a pressure-packed day and I can't cope with one more problem?

Intelligence, then, is a delicate blend of formal knowledge, common sense and coping strategies. This is not to say that the intelligent person is problem-free. Everyone has problems. It is how you deal with them that counts.

Don't be intimidated by the person with the big vocabulary or the high IQ or lots of initials after his or her name. And don't despair if your education doesn't measure up to someone else's. Remember, the intelligent person is the one who functions well and happily in this crazy, mixed-up world.

Your Record of Life's Journey

How often do you sit down at night and worry about your bills? How often do you agonize over your job or your health or your family? We all do. We feel it is our responsibility to take care of these things. But by over-concentrating on our concerns, we put a mental filter in place that screens out all but the bothersome areas of life.

What a feeling we get about life after a while! We begin to see only difficulty, doubt, and suspicion. At the extreme, we not only feel incapable of handling our trials, but we become afraid that others will exploit our weaknesses. The end result is a life full of fear and devoid of joy. That's a high price to pay for responsibility.

Fortunately, there is a lot more to life than problems. In fact, happiness coexists with difficulty; all we have to do is open our minds to it. Here is a simple exercise that can help do just that.

Keep a daily written account of the good things in your life. Yes, written. Thoughts are fleeting and easily changed. Write something good about each and every day, even if it is only that the shower delivered hot water. Watch those around you. Remember a special smile, an encouraging word, an insignificant favor someone did for you.

Write down your daily accomplishments: You did something you had been putting off. You confronted someone you feared. You stuck to your diet. Deliberately avoid recording the negative or frustrating parts of your day. Forget about the jerk who jammed up traffic, the waitress who forgot your side order, the operator who put you on hold and left you there. Life is full of these annoyances. But they are minor so why magnify them by dwelling on them?

Some negative things, however, do deserve mention in this journal. For instance, include problems after they have been solved. Life teaches her lessons the hard way sometimes, and we want to preserve those lessons to help us sidestep or cope with similar problems in the future. In effect what we record in our journals is victory over a difficult situation. A negative is turned into a strengthening positive.

By recording only the good things each day, you gradually train your eye to see in a more positive way. I am not advocating the use of rose-colored glasses or simplistic optimism. I am encouraging appreciation.

Besides changing your viewpoint, a positive daily record becomes a joyful history of your existence. As you read back over it, you find satisfaction and achievement. Your ability to capture such things now can help you sustain a hopeful attitude during difficult times. Life is both good and bad, happy and sad. By choosing which you concentrate on, you effectively decide whether you live in happiness or misery.

Stronger Together

You are good; I am, too. Imagine together what we could do.

We know that no man is an island and that with the help and support of others we can accomplish many wonderful things. Still, we often isolate ourselves in our worries, not wishing to trouble someone else or preferring to work through our challenges in private. We must resist this urge for we are, in fact, stronger together.

Maya Angelou, global Renaissance woman, is a beloved poet, novelist, educator, producer, actress, historian, film-maker, and civil rights activist. She writes:

> *The sisters and brothers you meet give you the materials which your character uses to build itself. It is said that some people are born great, others achieve it, some have it thrust upon them. In truth, the ways in which your character is built have to do with all three of those. Those around you, those you choose, and those who choose you..*

A Call for Grace, Patience, and Good Humor

We are called the Sandwich Generation, we Baby Boomers who are positioned between children and parents, both of whom look to us for support.

In some cases, this support consists of a sympathetic ear or a shoulder to cry on. But in others, the demands are far greater in terms of financial and physical support. According to the U.S. Bureau of the Census, 53 percent of males and 46 percent of females aged 18-24 lived at home in 2005. In the 25-34 year old category, 14 percent of men and eight percent of women lived at home that year.

On the other side of the equation, aging parents are requiring more support, too. The Bureau of Labor Statistics shows that in 2006, there were 767,000 personal and home care aides in the U.S. By 2016, they are projecting a 51 percent increase in the number of these jobs.

These are remarkable statistics, emerging at a time of tremendous pressure. Many women face the additional challenge of working full- or part-time jobs in a highly uncertain economy.

It is a daunting scenario. How are we to cope? We can start by quieting our minds and practicing a set of characteristics that allows us to feel sane, good, and sometimes even wise. Try grace, patience, and good humor.

Grace is a state of thoughtfulness toward others. Patience involves calmly tolerating delay, confusion, or inefficiency; enduring pain or trouble without losing self-control; and refusing to be provoked or angered by an insult or perceived slight. Good humor is the ability to see, appreciate, or express what is funny, amusing, ludicrous or ironic in a situation.

Yes, these terms are quaint—old-fashioned, curious, maybe even fanciful in our current society. But if there has ever been a time to learn and practice these characteristics it is now.

I have been thinking about this since my parents were here from Arizona for a rare, week-long visit this summer. As you might expect, there were many gatherings of family and friends and, since Mom and Dad were staying at my house, I was involved in most of them.

Planning began weeks before they arrived. The schedule of activities carried daily demands of time and attention. I fretted about my work. How could I take so much time off? How could I be with them and still fulfill professional obligations? How would I be ready to travel for business immediately after they left? How was I going to get everything done? Forget about grace!

I'll admit to feelings of mild resentment for siblings who were not investing the kind of resources I was, but who wanted time with Mom and Dad. What I realize in retrospect is the gift of perspective I gained over the days my parents were here.

The most poignant moment and stark reminder came from my father, who is struggling with Alzheimer's. The disease has progressed to the point where he did not remember sitting outside and marveling at fireflies for an hour one night. When we walked my dog the next day, I said I wondered if we would see fireflies again that evening.

Dad's reply: "Fireflies? What are those?"

I explained what they are in the same way I had a dozen times the evening before. He was charmed once again by my description and excited about the prospect of seeing them. "I don't think I've ever seen those."

I simply smiled and said maybe we'd be lucky.

It was a moment of sudden clarity in which I understood the extent of my mother's challenge and my father's mortality. It was a quiet moment that spoke volumes about what matters most.

As you struggle to manage too many demands on your time, attention, and resources, please remember grace, patience, and good humor. Magic happens when people make time to listen and care for each other. Memories get made. No credit history or technical skills are required.

A Quadruple Generation Gap!

When I was a kid, I remember hearing adults talk about a Generation Gap. The words were spoken with a 'big g' because it was a big deal.

I'm a Baby Boomer, so I'm tarred by association with the pot smoking, free-love, hippie crowd that surrounded me. But I lived in a strict middle-class household in which we had our mouths washed out with soap for saying words that pepper mainstream sit-coms today. Smoke pot? I was terrified of the stuff, not to mention what my parents would do to me if I even thought about experimenting with it.

There were big disconnects between my generation and my parents', but kids my age were gradually brought in line and we learned to accept some, though not all, of the rules and regulations we were taught. When it came to behavior on the job, we had little choice but to conform if we wanted to work and be promoted one day.

In retrospect, life was pretty simple then. Today we have quadruple the Gap with four generations at work. Attitudes and values have changed substantially over time and working together can sometimes feel nearly impossible.

Understanding what the world was like when each generation grew up helps to explain why people believe certain things and act the way they do. Mind you, broad generalizations can be dangerous because they never apply to everyone, but a big picture understanding can be useful.

Traditionalists, born between 1909 and 1945, grew up with the Great Depression, World War II, shortages of gas, sugar, and tires; and the Golden Age of Radio. Tarzan, the Lone Ranger, Babe Ruth and Joe DiMaggio were heroes. Traditional families and clear gender roles were supported by strong church and community ties. Saving for a rainy day was something everybody did while they worked hard and kept private lives private. Imagine that.

No so for the Baby Boomers, born between 1946 and 1964. Theirs was a time of chaos that played out, for the first time ever, on TV. Assassinations of John and Bobby Kennedy and Martin Luther King, Jr., Woodstock, the Civil Rights and Feminist movements, and the Vietnam war all screamed craziness! By contrast, Neil Armstrong's miraculous, eerily quiet walk on the moon seemed surreal. Money was easier to come by thanks to an economic expansion and personal gratification became the order of the day.

Gen X, born between 1965 and 1980, grew up as "latch-key kids." Their parents were sometimes separated, sometimes divorced, and almost always working. Globalization meant expanded markets, which in turn meant greater job demands that kept parents at work or away from home longer and longer. When the Challenger exploded on live TV, so did the romantic notion that astronauts were uber-humans, magically indestructible. Suddenly nothing seemed permanent or absolute; Gen X learned to be independent and self-sufficient.

For Millennials, or Gen Y, born after 1980, the world was all about technology, multiculturalism, and entrepreneurialism. The Internet brought an explosion of information and made the world a smaller, faster place. Today, electronic communication enables friendship across time zones and cultures and Gen Y embraces an inclusive, social justice view of diversity. They see problems created by earlier generations and are determined to do better. They feel little loyalty to employers—they've seen downsizing and the effects of global competition—and they spend money as fast as they earn it.

As we think about the progression of the world over the past four generations, it should be no surprise that we're experiencing gaps in our understanding of one another. Conflict between generations is as old as time. And somewhere in every generation is the person who shakes his or her head, convinced that we're all going to hell in a hand basket.

What matters in the end is that people take time to understand and appreciate differences, teach and expect behaviors that foster respect, and remember that all progress involves some pain. With this attitude in place, we can build bridges not only between generations, but far into the future.

Best You, Best Me

Have you ever wondered why, when you spend so much time and energy on self-improvement and positive thinking, no one seems to notice?

The biggest single reason for this is that everyone else is preoccupied with his or her own problems and responsibilities. It is possible, in fact, that everyone else is just as serious as you are about improving themselves—and just as inwardly focused.

Self-improvement requires immense concentration, motivation and self-appraisal. In many instances, it requires us to screen out the negative responses of others. We are often required to stand away from the crowd in order to stand for principles we believe in. It is not difficult to understand why, after a period of time, we can become highly motivated and self-improved isolates. By focusing on ourselves, we lose sight of others.

At this stage, perhaps we need to be reminded of a few basic but important facts. Everyone wants to feel important. Everyone wants to be noticed. Everyone wants to be appreciated.

Ask yourself this question: As you strive to become a better person, how much time do you spend noticing, appreciating and building up others? Do you recognize another's accomplishments? Do you appreciate another's talents or personal qualities? Do you thank others for their support? By helping others feel important and appreciated, you are helping yourself as well. Get someone to talk about his or her concerns or achievements and listen attentively. That person will consider you a sensitive and caring individual.

Let someone at work expound on a particular product or procedure, then make a few brief comments. You will be considered intelligent and capable. Ask a friend or family member for advice and thank that person for sharing his or her wisdom. You will be thought wise in return.

As you seek to improve yourself, remember that you cannot live effectively in isolation. Work at bringing out the best qualities in others and your own best qualities will shine.

Crabby? Try Encouragement

*H*ow did your day start today? Were you excited by its possibilities, pleased by its potential and generally in good spirits? Or did you rise only to mentally cloak yourself in armor, clench your fists, grit your teeth, and present a surly mug to fellow humans? What were your first thoughts about: pleasure or pain, opportunities or problems?

Very often the way you start your day is the way it generally progresses. If you start out bemoaning your many tasks and limited hours, you immediately feel pressured, constricted and doubtful of your capabilities. Your temperament is poor; your humor is bad. The day most certainly will not be one of your best.

One of the quickest, easiest and least expensive ways to head into a good day is to offer a bit of encouragement to someone near you. When you start the day with a genuine wish for another's happiness and well being, you trigger a positiveness of spirit that will make your own day more pleasant and productive.

No one has time to write a long letter but we all have time to jot a 30-second note. Imagine the surprise and joy of a friend who finds an email or, better yet, a hand-written note in his or her mailbox. It might say simply, "No time for news—just wanted you to know I'm thinking of you. Have a good day."

The same can be done with a quick before-the-rush phone call. Its purpose is to make contact and let a friend know that he or she is thought of today. Short, simple, and wonderful.

Sounds goody two-shoes you say? Sounds corny you sneer? When was the last time someone extended a wish for your happiness clear out of the blue? Perhaps never. For many of us that may be the sad truth.

Try a little bit of encouragement today. Don't be phony. Don't be embarrassed. Pick someone you know and like and give it a try. Be warm, be genuine, be sincere. You'll hear the happiness in the other's voice or you can imagine their delight in receiving your note.

Think of your act as an inexpensive, no-frills expression of goodwill that benefits the sender as much as the receiver.

Don't Run Alone!

S ometimes in our rushed and harried lives, we neglect things that had formerly been priorities. More specifically, relationship-oriented, feeling, sharing kinds of activities tend to get pushed aside in favor of long hours spent to advance career, education, or other personal goals. Isn't that a shame?

Many of our problems as professionals, scholars, or fast-tracking super-achievers tend to arise from a nagging sense that we may be losing our human touch, our ability to empathize with, relate to, and reach out to fellow human beings.

Here's a quick quiz to help you evaluate your empathy vs. efficiency quotient:

♦ You have made arrangements to meet a friend for lunch, but deadlines are staring you in the face. You: A) cancel your lunch date and work straight through your lunch hour; B) shrug your shoulders at the deadlines and go out to lunch; C) take a short break, meet your friend for coffee, then return to your work.

♦ You have put in long hours for the past month and your family is complaining that they never see you. You: A) reply in bad humor that the situation is unchangeable so they had better get used to it; B) chuck the long hours and oppressive responsibility at work (you're not appreciated anyway); C) explain the situation and ask your family for their patience as you work your way through it.

Obviously, these responses represent extremes, and there is a middle ground. The fever of professionalism, efficiency and excellence that has swept the business world and academia of late needs some tempering.

We need people, you and I. And whether we realize it or not, there are many people supporting us, caring for us and comforting us when we fall short of our ambitions. Let's look at those important others with full appreciation. Let's make time for them in our busy lives. And let's always be grateful that when we are in full stride, they run to catch up with us every once in a while to let us know we are not running alone.

Mom, Dad, family, and friends, thank you. Though I run frantically sometimes, I know you are there. And you are precious, every one.

Energy, Meet Experience

Take kindly the counsel of the years, gracefully surrendering the things of youth.

hese words are from *Desiderata*, copyrighted by Max Ehrmann in 1927. They are more appropriate today than ever before. We live in a youth-oriented society. Baby Boomers have hit full stride and whiz kids wield unheard of power. Children ignore their parents (what's new?), students reject their teachers' lessons, and the young guy at the office scorns the old (and tired) veteran. Our preoccupation with surface beauty and the fit physique threatens to make ours a shallow and short-lived society. Disrespect for the elderly is widespread and shameful.

It is time for youth to put smugness aside and listen to the wisdom of elders. We have so much to gain. We know that experience is the finest teacher but must this experience be personal? Or can we learn from others?

Think back on the many things you have learned in your lifetime. If you are lucky, you have learned how to perform innumerable tasks, talk with people, solve problems and look out for yourself. Is your education in life complete? No. Add ten or twenty or thirty years to your present age. Imagine all the things you will do in that time, the places you will visit, the challenges you will meet. Of course you will be wiser and stronger. You will have grown.

We have much to learn from those who are older than we are. And they have much to share. The next time you are tempted to scorn someone as old-fashioned, out of it, or feeble-minded, stop a minute and listen. Though times have changed and values with them, the problems of life remain fairly constant.

Let's learn to combine the wisdom and experience of the elderly with the energy and enthusiasm of youth. It's a partnership that could yield spectacular results.

Happiness in Perspective

We humans spend a lot of time complaining about the hassles of life and trying to find ways to make life easier and happier. Perhaps we need to stop and ask a few questions. Is there someone in your life who cares about you? Someone who will listen to your ideas and offer suggestions? Do you have food in the fridge? Clothes to clean? Some place to care for and call your own? My goodness, you're lucky!

Do you have time to think about and plan your life? Are you able to work for the resources that will help make your dreams come true? Do you breathe evenly, hear adequately and feel the countless textures encountered by your fingertips each day? Again, by gosh, you're lucky.

It's true that these kinds of things evoke a "so what" response from many of us. And it is these very things—rich blessings all—that are the first to be taken for granted when our sights are set on greater goals.

But you know as well as I do that in order to accomplish big things, we need to start small. And we always start with the basics. But once we have basics and so much more, why do we continue to want? Why are we constantly looking for happiness? Could it be that in acquiring more and more things we are squeezing out happiness? Is there a solution?

Learn to appreciate what you have. That's step number one to contentment. Next, consider how you might make life better for someone else. Thinking in this manner encourages us to make responsible use of the things we have. It makes life more than just a time to accumulate materials and wonder what we missed.

Think about what you could share, be it time, money or knowledge that could improve another person's outlook on life. Do you have a word of encouragement to give? Could you refer someone to a job opening you know about? Do you have special knowledge or insight that could make a difference to someone you know?

It is in sharing our gifts that we begin to see just how fortunate we are. And it is in helping another that we learn the joy of giving.

Are you unhappy with life? Maybe you need to turn away from everything that's wrong with it and discover all that's right. Maybe you also need to think about using what you have to make someone else happier. "It is more blessed to give than to receive." We know this is true. Let's try to practice its meaning—and practice our way to happiness.

Kindness is Healing

Kindness is a virtue fast disappearing in today's rough-and-tumble, dog-eat-dog, I'm-taking-care-of-me-first world. Nowhere is the lack of kindness more evident than in our homes. Divorce, battered women and abused children provide tragic testimony to our declining concern for kindness.

There are other smaller indicators as well. Poor manners, mean-tempered remarks and the single-minded determination to succeed all reflect our lack of concern for others.

We have adopted a new frankness with one another over the past decade as well. Assertiveness training has enabled us to speak our minds more freely. We demand, criticize and insist with much more vigor than ever before. The power politics of large corporations cultivate this assertiveness and leave little room for kindness.

Today we also know about "problem ownership." This concept says that if you have a problem with something I say or do, well, it's your problem. You own your thoughts, which in turn dictate your feelings. Hence, you own any problem you might choose to have regardless of what I do.

There are many techniques available today to help us feel freer of worry, guilt and other emotions that threaten our happiness. Many of them are to be applauded, for too many of us spend far too much time in the grasp of worry and remorse. And yet, by concentrating solely on our feelings, our concerns, and our freedoms, we isolate ourselves from the rest of humanity. And because in isolation there is no sharing, in isolation there is no happiness.

Are you feeling lonely? Left out? Lost? Have you been bruised by the unkind actions of others? Try extending a little kindness to someone you know.

Kindness can be so simple to practice. Stop and listen to someone instead of hurrying on to your next task. Congratulate someone's success instead of envying it. Accept an apology instead of cultivating your hurt. Give away a free smile, a gentle touch, a kind word. Not only will your kindness help others through a dark or difficult day, but their gratitude (and possibly surprise) will bring new light and warmth to your day as well.

Learn to Trust Again

S pecialization became a byword of the 1980s. It was pervasive in the worlds of science, academics and business, spawning the appearance of subject matter experts. To a large degree, specialization enabled man to achieve far more than he would have if, for instance, all doctors had remained general practitioners.

But as in most things, specialization can have undesirable effects as well. Individuals may withdraw into their own areas of expertise, creating a sort of tunnel vision that obscures a bigger picture. Each specialist believes that his field is the most important. Competition for scarce resources intensifies. Cooperation and understanding fly out the window. Lines of communication rarely coincide and so become lost in the wilderness. Obviously, the creation of a multitude of islands is sadly counterproductive.

Leo Buscaglia, Ph.D., professor of education at USC and much sought after lecturer, addresses this concern in his 1985 book, *Living, Loving and Learning*. "We've ceased caring. We've formed little tight nuclei. We say, 'These are the things I must be concerned about. It's not my concern what goes on out there.'

"I think you've arrived when you recognize that not a leaf falls without it in some way affecting you. There's no place to hide anymore! The boss yells at you. You go home and yell at your husband or wife. Your husband or wife smacks out at the kid. The kid kicks the dog that bites that cat that urinates on the rug.

"Where did it start! I need you and we better get back to group affiliation, to being able to give up a little bit in order to get. We've got to learn to trust again, believe again, and work together again."

Decades later, we say "Amen."

Necessity is the Mother of Invention

*T*his truism, thought to have come originally from Plato, is once again in vogue. Tough times can produce ingenious solutions if we approach them with the proper mindset.

No one welcomes necessity. It limits choices, raises anxiety, and saps energy. Necessity forces change, sometimes urgent change. This need for change inspires invention.

I remember as a young girl—one of six children growing up in a small, middle-class community—having inventive meals like egg noodles and baked beans, and stirring dye tablets into bowls of white oleo margarine.

Family vacations were often low-budget affairs that found the entire family stuffed into an old station wagon rambling north for a week's worth of fishing, rowing around small lakes, and playing tetherball at the community beach.

Clothes were hand-me-downs that embarrassed me sometimes. Shoes lasted at least a year, even longer when our feet stopped growing. We had one pair apiece.

With little money, no electronic games, and no notion of mother-arranged play dates, we were left to fend for ourselves when it came to entertainment. A carpeted stairway from the first to the second floor became a slide. Imagine six youngsters, toddler through third grade, sliding on bellies amidst shrieks of laughter. Before we perfected our technique, there were plenty of bumped chins and a rug burn or two, but we were undeterred.

When we bored of this, we would sit around looking at one another until a twinkle arose in someone's eye and we'd all grin in anticipation of the next adventure. We rarely stopped moving.

Thinking back on those austere times, I realize that we learned how to "read" each other and use our imaginations. When we called out, "I'm bored," Mom simply said, "Find something to do." Inevitably, we did.

Many years later, as a single mom struggling to provide for two daughters of my own, I wanted to find some "fun" in our plight. The girls didn't know how bad things were and I didn't want them to know I was scared. So I devised a game we called "Survival." Not very creative, I'll admit, but certainly descriptive. And it preceded Reality TV by more than a decade!

Our game consisted of meal preparation using only the ingredients immediately on hand in cupboard, freezer, or fridge. I shake my head to think of some of the concoctions we whipped up. On more than a few occasions, popcorn was the main dish, consumed in front of a favorite TV show or over long, exploratory conversations about boys, school, and life. In retrospect, we had a ball.

Today's economic situation is a truly scary crisis for many. There is little to capture our imaginations when we fret over real survival. Yet new ways of managing austerity are springing up once again. Recipes, crafts, home decorations, and entertaining are simpler and in many cases, more satisfying.

It's no surprise that women are at the center of this new, inventive era—necessity is the mother of invention, after all. We have always been caregivers, nurturers, and feeders of families. This important role, while perhaps never valued properly, is making a comeback. Rachel Ray has picked up where Martha Stewart left off.

My point is not to suggest that hardship be shrugged off. No one is in the mood to yuck it up over difficult choices. Rather, I'd like to suggest that trying times have the potential of creating important memories and teaching worthwhile lessons.

One of these lessons is to avoid comparing your difficulties to someone else's. As *Desiderata* reminds us, "If you compare yourself with others, you may become vain or bitter, for always there will be greater and lesser persons than yourself."

Here is another reminder: As adults go, so go children. If adults can find ways to manage disappointment, accept new realities, and offer a smile and a hug once in a while, kids can learn that hardship is manageable. And if we're lucky, we may get to look back a few years down the road and find reason to smile about what we created.

Share You!

Congratulations. You, as a human being, have the unique and wonderful opportunity to share. And by sharing, to teach, entertain and encourage people around you.

There are many forms of sharing. We are taught at a young age to share toys and food; as we grow older, we are encouraged to share feelings, especially those of anger or sorrow. The benefits of sharing are many; especially well known is the therapeutic value of sharing emotions.

Yet many of us hesitate to share. We keep our feelings hidden because we fear the vulnerability that results from personal disclosure. We guard new or specialized information to keep a competitive edge over others. We protect our material assets even as we work to acquire more.

Despite this hesitancy to share, we do know that we feel better as we get closer to others. Each of us has a need to feel understood, accepted and valued, not for what we have but for who we are. Doesn't it make sense, then, to open up and give of ourselves at every opportunity? We can train ourselves to do this, but we must start small and allow the process to be a gradual one.

Share a laugh, a handshake, an incident. Share a favorite book or TV show. Share an experience. Invite someone who has never gone fishing to join your next expedition. Teach him the sport and enjoy the time together. Use the time to share stories, opinions and information.

Remember, too, that there is one and only one you. There has never been, nor will there ever be, another person just like you. That in itself is an incredible fact, and an exceptional reason to share joyfully all that you are. By sharing, you give the world the chance to know, understand, appreciate and love you. It's a neat payoff for a fun activity.

The Gift that Keeps on Giving

'Tis the season once again for wracking your brain without wrecking your budget as you search for the best gifts for your family, friends and business associates.

Here are some ideas culled from Oprah and Amazon that offer something for just about everyone: scrapbooking materials, a toothbrush sanitizer, candles, cookbooks, make-up, a gravity inversion table for sore backs, pedometer, perfect pushup devices, puzzles, tire gauge, weather radio, digital camera, flash drive, computer and cookware.

Most women I know enter the holiday season filled with the desire to make it special. They want their loved ones to be happy and they take great pains to provide just the right gift, delicious meal, favorite treat, or other seasonal delight to bring a twinkle to the eye of their loved ones.

But somehow the magic doesn't always happen. The busier and more crowded the season, the less time loved ones have to appreciate their gifts. With so much stuff coming at them, it's hard to muster the energy to be excited about a new gadget or pretty sweater. Women end up feeling disappointed or hurt by this wan appreciation and wonder why they knock themselves out year after year. Not to mention the strain on their budgets!

May I suggest a new approach this holiday season? Think of yourself as the gift that keeps on giving. Now before you roll your eyes or laugh yourself silly, let's examine this idea.

Imagine the difference you could make by offering the gift of your time and attention, not just for the day, but for the whole year ahead. A homemade coupon book filled with loving promises is inexpensive to create and easy to customize for the recipient.

For a teenager, you might offer a monthly pizza or burger night out. Of course this would have to be good only during the week; what teenager wants to be seen with Mom on the weekend? Included in the evening is your undivided attention for a conversation about whatever your teen wants to explore. Your job is to notice what's neat about your kid and pay close attention to it. The expiration date is the last day of the month each month and you should follow up to be sure you schedule it.

Your teen may think this is weird at first, but when you make this date as important as a monthly budget meeting at work, she will begin to see that she matters.

In the same fashion, you can offer a monthly one-on-one meeting to your direct reports at work. The rules of engagement are the same: they get your undivided attention; you get to learn what's on their minds. As a side benefit, you may find those annoying "got-a-minute?" meetings begin to disappear.

You might offer your friends the chance to share a favorite meal each month. Or take a favorite road trip, see a favorite movie, or play a favorite board game. Get creative!

There are a million little things you do that nobody else can do in the same way.

Share your reassuring touch, soft smile, that twinkle in your eye, the strong shoulder or generous ear. Listen without comment to a friend's rant, then ask how you can help. Endure with good humor the story you've heard fourteen times already from your spouse. Call good morning to the kids as they rumble into the kitchen for breakfast. Share the news or weather report that you heard before anyone else was up.

At work, keep your wits about you when everyone else is panicking. Clean up the coffee spill in the break room even though you didn't make the mess. Turn gossip to more productive conversation.

A creative coupon book is a tangible gift of promises. Yes, it will require a true commitment of time. But as you fulfill your promises each month, you will be rewarded with newly enriched relationships and a growing bank of memories. Talk about a gift that keeps on giving! Happy, happy holidays!

The Greatest Tribute

S et this book aside for a moment right now and think about the people who have most influenced your life. That's right, do it now. Who has most influenced your life?

After defining that person or persons, move them to the back of your mind and call forward the vital lessons you have learned. I don't mean to suggest that the people are not important. They are, and we'll address them in a minute. But first, answer the question, "What did this important person or persons teach you?"

I have learned a myriad of lessons from a diverse and completely unrelated group of individuals. The lessons have included perseverance, toughness, pride, determination, self-acceptance, tolerance, cheerfulness and most importantly, love. Not the handholding, heart-pounding, highly sensual love that is peddled on today's market. But rather, the kind of love that trusts, forgives, accepts and rejoices despite imperfections and shortcomings.

The lessons I have learned have helped me to deal with disappointment, loss, misunderstanding and, on the other end of the spectrum, over-enthusiasm. Not surprisingly, most of my teachers have had years of experience to share. However, children have taught me a thing or two as well. Our learning depends upon our receptiveness.

Now, after considering the lessons, bring back to mind the people who have influenced you. How did they live? What were their attitudes? Did you feel comfortable baring your soul to these people? Did you trust them to help you strengthen your weaknesses rather than exploiting these weaknesses for their gain? How did they interact with others? List, in concrete terms, the qualities these people had that made you want to emulate them.

Chances are, such qualities were people skills you would like to have. They listened, they heard, they interpreted based on their experiences, they offered suggestions, and they allowed you to mull over their input and make your own decision.

Such individuals likely possessed several important characteristics:

- The ability to listen without passing judgment.
- The ability to empathize.
- The ability to sort through experiences and make appropriate suggestions based on your problems.
- The ability to withhold a sermon that would have gone unheeded.
- The ability to allow you to choose your own path.

Let's salute those who have guided our lives toward positive goals. Let's thank them from the heart with the greatest tribute we can pay—a life based on the positive lessons we have learned from them. Let's emulate our teachers in the hope of one day having the chance to help those who might look to us for answers.

The Magic of Noticing

Would you like a simple, inexpensive, convenient way to make someone you care about very happy? Notice him or her. That's right, notice. And comment.

When someone in your household looks especially nice, say so. And say why. Is it clothing, hairstyle, attitude? Maybe this person is excited about an event taking place that day. Ask about it; comment on it. When a friend does something for you, whether it be great or small in scope, say thank you. Specifically name the thing you are grateful for and how it helped you.

Notice the shine of someone's hair, the twinkle in another's eye, the jauntiness of someone's walk. Appreciate rich laughter, recognize a profound thought, respond to an enthusiastic idea. Be aware of how unique each person is. Realize that there is one, and only one, of each person in this world. That makes billions of different, interesting people living today in the same world as you. You cannot know or appreciate most of these individuals, but you can value those close to you. Why not let them know it?

One of the most effective ways of showing someone you care is to be aware when that person is near you. If you are conversing with someone and this person walks by, extend a hand. Catch his or her eye across the room, toss a wink. These things are so simple to do, yet the effects can be magical. Think of how delighted you are when you have the full attention of someone else, and the joy you feel at being unexpectedly noticed. Your regard for the other person increases; you value him or her more.

Imagine how human relations around the world could be improved by extending small gestures. By noticing people around us—and telling them so—we spark within them a wonderful feeling of worth and a desire to reciprocate the favor.

Two Steps to Effective Living

*T*hroughout the ages, there have been lots of formulas suggested for effective living. Some of these formulas have been long and complicated; others have been short and perhaps a bit simplistic. The complicated ones require a lot of time and effort, but justify themselves by reminding us that we only get out of life what we put into it. The short ones offer a quick-fix approach to happier living.

The formula I propose for living better consists of just two basic steps. First, discover what your talents are. Second, feel the responsibility to use these talents to the fullest to benefit someone else.

Discovering what your talents are sounds like a simple task. But think of all the people who influence this process. Parents begin shaping children at an early age by praising certain skills and ignoring others. Teachers and guidance counselors point students in directions they deem to be most appropriate. Friends and acquaintances may see something that others have missed and point it out as a special gift. The job market, too, can influence our decisions about which skills to develop. The inputs are many and it is easy to become confused.

Why is it important to discover what your talents are? Look around you at the numbers of people who dislike their jobs but keep them anyway. They are largely unexcited, unfulfilled and unhappy. Chances are their performance at work is mediocre. Would these people be happier if they had the opportunity to use their special talents? One can only guess, but I would guess they would be.

Step number two in the formula is to feel the responsibility to use your talents to benefit someone else. This step might appear naïve or simplistic. However, in order to feel responsible for effectively using your skills, you must first be grateful for having been blessed with them. Humility is implicit in this gratitude. Also, the world around you encourages you to search for ways to parlay your skills into greater personal wealth or recognition. "Me first" thinking is far more common than "others first" concern. But using your talents to benefit others provides a bigger purpose for your work. It is a mature, secure way of thinking that is all too rare in our society.

Be thankful for the skills you have been given. Seek ways to expend yourself in the service of others, improving your skills as you go. There is great satisfaction in working to your limit in an area in which you are specially qualified. A greater satisfaction comes in witnessing the joy of someone who has benefited from your action.

Why We Need Generations of Women at Work

*H*appy Mother's Day! Our celebrations today may be a little different than when my siblings and I made homemade cards at school and burnt toast on Mother's Day Sunday. Families don't have the luxury of time together like we once did. Now mothers and daughters are far more likely to work outside the home and celebrate the day with Hallmark cards and cell phone calls; it's all we have time for!

Reflecting on this turned my thoughts to the fact that mothers and daughters share a work world that is different, too. Used to be, the spats between generations occurred mostly at home over kitchen counters or in family rooms. Now they bubble up in workplaces and seem more confusing because someone's mom might report to someone's daughter. Though we hate to admit it, the old order of "age over beauty" made some sense.

But in mourning what's wrong, we lose the chance to find something very right and exciting about blending multiple generations at work.

Remember that first job fresh out of school? At last, an adult adventure with paychecks to support adult choices: a new apartment, a car (maybe new, probably not), cute clothes and stylish shoes, a social life. The excitement and energy of youth is essential for fueling progress at work. And yet, sometimes that energy drives an attitude that's a bit annoying.

A little further along the career path might find additional loved ones sharing your life. A partner, perhaps children, new friends. Each new person brings added responsibility and a demand on your time. The world looks a little different than it did just a decade earlier.

As a parent, you may experience increasing financial pressure. On top of food and clothing come school costs, athletic team fees, toys, computers, cell phones. Additionally, where you might once have been accused of having an attitude, you now find your children developing their own!

As family pressures increase, demands of the job continue to rise, as well. You may find you get less sleep at precisely the time you need more. And the people who used to be reasonable at work have suddenly become needy or overtly competitive with you. What is going on here?

Gail Sheehy became famous for her 1976 book, *Passages*, in which she outlined the "predictable crises of adult life" and wrote about the adjustments required to manage them. Her later work, *New Passages*, compresses some of the time between crises and admits that today's world makes them feel even more intense than when she first identified them.

All of which points to the fact that we need multiple generations of women at work. Why? Because without the energy of youth, we might tire before our contributions have been a) made and b) acknowledged. This is no small point.

We also need older women, even elders, to help us understand that mistakes are survivable, that energy must be preserved, and that sometimes the thoughts that scream so loudly in our heads need not necessarily come out of our mouths. This, too, is no small point.

The problem with multiple generations—and it has been written about since the beginning of time, probably in hieroglyphics on cave walls—is that we just can't seem to get along. Young women think older women are stuck in their ways, not to mention embarrassingly unstylish at times. Older women think young women have a lot to learn, even with college degrees and advanced computer skills. And so it is.

But there's a bigger story and a greater opportunity. Partnering across generations encourages new thinking while it leverages lessons learned. Imagine that each of us sits in a different seat in the arena of life. Imagine that this arena rotates, like a revolving restaurant. What we see—and know—in one moment can be different the next. When we set the table with patience and tolerance, and join one another to listen and share, our ideas are richer, our contributions more meaningful. That's a Mother's Day wish we can all share!

Gaining Perspective

*L*ife has a way of shrinking us, sometimes. We get so caught up in everyday chaos that we lose the bigger picture. We battle the little stuff and forget about the big stuff. We don't mean to, it's just that...Well, there are many reasons.

Funny, too, how we take certain things with great seriousness and argue with passionate vigor about what is right or wrong. But Marcus Aurelius reminds us:

> *Everything we hear is an opinion, not a fact.*
> *Everything we see is a perspective, not the truth.*"

Marcus Aurelius was a Roman emperor and author of Meditations, a famous tome of Stoic philosophy written in Greek. A Stoic believed that only virtue is good, only vice is bad, and the things with which we busy ourselves are all indifferent. Imagine!

A Woman's Paradox

*I*f you've heard it once, you've probably heard it a hundred times: If you want to get ahead, you must learn to say no. You cannot be all things to all people. You cannot make everyone happy. Saying no can be exceedingly difficult! Learning how is essential.

But wait. What about *carpe diem*!? Seize the day!? We are urged to live in the moment, hold nothing back, and reach for every opportunity that presents itself. After all, one never knows where the road less traveled may lead.

Life is filled with paradox and this is one of the most vexing for women. We enjoy saying yes. It is an affirmation, a declaration of willingness to experience life and to help where we are needed. People admire and appreciate us when we say yes. They smile at us. Good feelings are shared.

Yet, you know you cannot say yes to everyone who requests your time or every opportunity that arises. Try as you might, your time and energy are limited. There really is only so much you can do.

Women around the world struggle with this paradox. Saying no seems so churlish. Surely you could find a way to participate if you really wanted to. In saying no are you selfish? Lazy? Perhaps you feel guilty when you turn someone away or decline an invitation. If only there was a way to be more certain.

Rest assured, you are not alone in your feelings.

While certainty is an illusion, one key to making yes/no decisions with grace and pride is having a sense of where you want your life to go. Knowing what matters to you, what satisfies you, who you want to spend time with, the experiences you want to have, the things you want to learn, and the aspects of yourself you want to share are critical elements. Taking time to figure this out is a challenge unto itself!

Many women are encouraged throughout their formative years to be responsive to the needs of others. "Women are nurturers," says society. We are, and I would hate to see women abdicate this honorable and important role. It sustains families and communities. Imagine where your children, friends, spouse or partner would be without you!

Yet the conflicting voice, which gathers volume year to year, is the one that says, "Go for the gusto! Be all you can be. Find your passion. Live today. Follow your dreams." It is a romantic voice that sometimes feels as though it has little to do with daily reality. Yet it fills us with energy and hope.

It takes a strong woman to know her mind, heart, and soul and construct her life according to her talents, passions, and dreams. Passion means different things to different women at different stages of life. It can refer to love, marriage, and a family. It can mean supporting a philanthropic cause. It can mean striking out on your own to do that which is rarely done.

Whatever you decide, it is important to recognize that you cannot do everything at once. We live life in chapters. Choices made in the past may carry implications for your life today. Choosing to be a parent, taking a promotion at work, maintaining or severing a relationship, enrolling in a course of study, altering your lifestyle through diet and exercise, changing careers, moving to a new town or state—these and many other life choices bring responsibilities that shape our days. They all require energy.

When you set goals that define your life's journey, it is easier to choose the things that support your vision while turning away from those that distract.

And while it is true that you cannot see around the next corner and what matters to you today may be different tomorrow, you do know, in your private moments, what matters most. Honoring your deepest dreams and allocating time and energy to work toward them gives you the energy and optimism you need to help selected others.

One final thought: As you consider this paradox, please remember that unless you can say no, you never really say yes.

Bad Girls at Work

I have had the privilege of speaking to the Waukesha County Chamber Women's Professional Development Network numerous times. One topic, "Women Bullying Women," created quite a stir.

My own ire on the subject was raised by a *New York Times* article that described a formal questionnaire designed by professors of two prominent universities that asked women to keep track of how many times in a six-month period they are bullied by other women. How ridiculous, I thought. Why focus women's attention on the slights they perceive from co-workers and draw it away from learning about the business? No wonder women have trouble being taken seriously.

My irritation prompted me to learn more. I read several books on bullying, talked with a wide range of women in business and nonprofit organizations, and contacted the Institute on Workplace Bullying. That such an organization exists at all is sad.

I learned that bullying behavior often starts among girls in grade school. (Moms, pay attention.) It is frequently silent in its execution and it can scar women for years. It continues at work where women with poor self-confidence use the tools of silent aggression—rumors, social exclusion, "the silent treatment," and seemingly innocent personal criticism—to bully colleagues. The research gave me an appreciation for the subtlety of this behavior, and its pervasiveness.

Insecurity and poor self-esteem are the leading causes of bullying, though no bully would ever admit to this. Competition—for high-visibility projects, attention from powerful leaders, and a chance to look smart in front of peers—is another primary trigger for bullies.

What should you do if you experience this silent aggression, hostile rumors or cliques of women who seek to discredit and isolate you at work?

Recognize it for what it is and choose not to participate. Do not give your time or attention to behavior that distracts you from doing exceptional work. Yes, doing exceptional work can make you a target, especially if you happen to work with insecure people.

But recognize that this bad behavior is not about you. It is about them. When bullies cannot light you up in indignation or get you to protect yourself, they move on to another target. Dismissing their nonsense is the right thing to do. And it is the most difficult thing to do.

Most women who bully are accomplished at the practice! They know how to zing others in little ways that seem innocent on the surface, but cut in destructive ways. For example, a simple comment, "Nice shoes," issued with a smirk or raised eyebrow will cause the recipient to wonder if she looks like a dork. I know, I've experienced this very thing!

It is difficult to feel strong and self-assured walking into an important meeting if you're feeling bad about your shoes. Or hair. Or handbag. It takes great self-control—and practice—to put this nagging little thought out of your mind and choose to focus on the content of the meeting instead.

When you can do this successfully and consistently, you will frustrate the bully. She may escalate her attacks in the short run to see if she can take you down another way. Remember, she is skilled. Keep going about your business and in time she will find an easier target.

You can also help yourself by observing the bully in action with others. You will see quickly that the bully's bad behavior is in fact all about her, not you.

Ultimately, your best strategy is to promise yourself each day to be the most accomplished and gracious woman you know how to be; a woman of true substance. Then do everything in your power to keep your promise to yourself.

You'll have days when the bully gets the better of you. None of us is a constant paragon of virtue. Forgive yourself and move on.

Here is an important truth: You cannot change a bully's behavior, but you can change your responses to it. Focus your energy and attention on making yourself better and stronger each day. You'll build pride in yourself and the bad girls will find someone else to pick on.

Can You Have It All?

dvertisers, self-help gurus, even well meaning friends tell us that if we want things badly enough and put our minds to it, we can have it all.

When you have it all, you are beautiful, smart, funny, wealthy and successful in everything you try. You have a fantastic figure that you dress in designer clothing. You drive a sexy car that rests overnight in an expansive garage adjoining your home, which could be featured in the pages of *Architectural Digest*. Your kitchen is equipped with every modern cooking accessory and your favorite restaurants are but a smart phone touch away. Your husband is handsome and popular and your children, if you have any, are model students and community servants. You love and care for each of them with gentleness, patience and joy. In turn, you are loved and admired by people you have never met.

In addition to these wonderful gifts, all of your private dreams have come true. Your life is perfect.

Are you laughing yet? Is it possible to have it all?

This question came up in an earnest group discussion recently. Women really want to know what they can expect from life! As I listened to the banter, it occurred to me that different women have different ideas about what "all" is.

One young woman wants to work long hours for the next year to assure promotion at her company. She believes that when this happens she will have the kind of position she wants with enough money to buy a house and furnish it according to her taste. She is not interested in having a family, at least not now.

Another woman has a family that is mostly grown. She wants more time to travel and pursue recreational hobbies. Her husband is not adventuresome, so she would like a handsome travel partner, who knows his way around the world.

Still another woman wants a home in the Catskills, horses to ride, groom hands to tend them, and a hot tub in the back yard. She would drink fine champagne, eat organic foods, and have both a hairdresser and a personal trainer. Her clothing would be custom designed and her wardrobe would be updated each season.

The notion of having it all generates different visions for different women. For each generation, the possibilities are different because the world is different.

Circumstances and cultural values have a way of shifting, sometimes dramatically. These shifts offer new ways of looking at the world and the self within it.

Still, "having it all" suggests ease, a bounty of material goods and a lifestyle that is bigger and better than what you currently have. Having it all means being perfectly fulfilled.

At this point someone asked, "Who are we to even think we could have it all?" She said her life would never be so expansive or luxurious. She cited lottery winners who won tons of money only to end up poor again after spending wildly as proof that some people are meant to have more than others. She spoke of contentment.

For her, having it all means appreciating the people who share her life. She enjoys time spent with friends and feels happy every night to go to sleep near her family. This woman takes delight in seeing Mother Nature's mood each morning and in listening to the earliest thoughts on the minds of her husband and two children. For her, each day is new and different, showing her something she had not seen before whether it's a twinkle in her son's eye or a tiny air hole in a piece of toast.

The truth is that "having it all," means something uniquely different to each of us. It often changes as life unfolds. Craft your list carefully. Be sure to say no to those things that others may say you should want but don't hold any significance for you.

What do you want and what are you willing to do to get it? Both the wish and the work, undertaken in a spirit of appreciation, bring fulfillment.

Decisions, Decisions

How many times have you made a decision, reconsidered, reverse your decision, then changed your mind again? How many times have you made a decision and stuck with it, but wondered for days and weeks afterward if it was the right decision? Everyone who has done these things knows that indecision and uncertainty are exhausting.

Why do we torment ourselves in this way, especially when we know from first-hand experience how much energy is wasted through doubting? There are several reasons.

First, we may be over-anxious about making the right decision. We often feel the eyes of everyone around us fixed upon us, watching to see whether we succeed or fail. We need to remember always that success comes from doing. Even though a decision may turn out unfavorably, we generally have the chance to correct course later on. Also, incorrect decisions can be helpful in sharpening our thinking and decision making skills.

Another reason we have a hard time sticking with a decision is because we have too many options, some with conflicting consequences. This may result from having unclear goals or from trying to satisfy too many people. The solution here is to figure out—and write down—who and what are most important to you.

When faced with a decision, take out your list. Consider your alternatives in light of the effects each will have upon those most important people and things. Some choices will be obviously better than others, so deciding becomes easier.

Sometimes we vacillate in our decision making simply because we are not sure what we want the outcome to be. We want more information and some assurances about the future. We wish for a crystal ball or some sign from heaven. And we decide and re-decide as we wait for that unmistakable sign. All of which is exhausting! We need to learn how to do our thinking, doubting and struggling before a decision is made.

Then, once we choose, we must have the courage to stick with our judgment. If it turns out incorrectly, we can modify the outcome with a future decision. No one is right all the time. No one expects you to be, either.

Each time you're faced with a difficult decision, follow this plan: Gather all available information. Consider your options and the consequences of each choice. Make a decision. Vow to stick with it.

It looks easy, but it requires determination. By practicing this method, you will become a stronger person and a better decision maker. You'll also sleep better at night.

Don't Doubt, Do.

"I can't do that. I don't know how."

We have heard that excuse often—from kids, from friends; why, we have even said it ourselves. And it's legitimate. If we don't know how to do something, we can't very well do it. Yes, legitimate. Once.

After you use this excuse once, it is used up for a particular activity. Learn how. Find someone to teach you. Make the effort even though you may feel it won't be worth it. Maybe it will.

Chances are you're afraid you won't be very good at it, which is why you haven't bothered to learn. Perhaps you're afraid of doing it incorrectly and suffering embarrassment. Maybe you're afraid of all-out failure and total humiliation. Do it anyway. If you hurt someone, apologize. Otherwise, grin and bear it. We can all appreciate a rueful smile and a shrug; we've all been there. Chalk it up and move on. Remember: "A man's errors are what make him amiable." (Goethe wrote that.)

Never adopt the attitude: "See, I told you I couldn't do it." Doing (or attempting to do) is more important than succeeding. Doing is growing. Doing is learning. Doing is what counts.

Consider Shakespeare's words:

> *Our doubts are traitors*
> *And make us lose the good we oft might win*
> *By fearing to attempt.*

In plain English—no guts, no glory!

Escape Ruts with Recombination

You and I are creatures of habit. We tend to shape the patterns of our lives by using the same bits of information over and over again in the same ways. We perform tasks in manners that have become routine. We keep company with the same people. We go again and again to the places that have become familiar to us. We have the same food for breakfast each morning and read the newspaper at a particular time each day.

Security and predictability in a changing world are the benefits of such behavior and we sometimes cling to our habits simply to define who we are. "I wear black socks, not green."

But boredom and discontent are the uncomfortable side effects of habit. Despite our need for security, we also have a longing for deep feeling, for challenge, for fun. We bemoan the ruts we get into.

Is there a solution to this apparent either/or problem? Yes. It is called recombination. Recombination is simply taking the same bits of information and combining them in different ways to find new patterns, new methods and new possibilities. Because we use information we already have, there is little danger of going too far astream or getting lost in the new patterns we create.

By recombining the pieces of our lives in new ways, we begin the process of asking new questions and discovering new possibilities. Recombination sparks curiosity and leads to discovery. The process feeds itself as pleasurable new experiences promote further experimentation. Recombination can help us build new confidence in our choices, a new attitude toward change and, ultimately, a new and more interesting life.

Of course, recombination requires a breaking of habit and a deviation from the normal way of doing things, but you can begin with something as simple as your wardrobe. Wear a different shirt with a particular pair of pants. Change a blouse/skirt combination. Add different accessories. Try new colors.

As you become more comfortable with small changes, expand your recombining efforts. Think about problems in alternative ways. Sit in a different seat during a weekly meeting. Take a new route to work. Eat dessert for breakfast. Try to apply knowledge you have in one area to other situations. If you have cracked the code on a recalcitrant teenager, apply your learning to a challenging boss or colleague.

Learn to realize that the bits and pieces of your life can be shaped into a variety of patterns simply by changing the ways they are put together. Discovery awaits!

Get Organized!

O rganization is one of the primary keys to success. The importance of organization in business is evidenced by the scores of workshops, seminars and books devoted to the subject. Consumer magazines also offer numerous articles on how to organize our lives, both business and personal.

The techniques of organizing are many and varied. From the creation of a master plan to scheduling five-minute sprint sessions, our lives can be cut up, broken down, and then restructured into more efficient and effective entities.

Experts on the subject cite many benefits to organization. An organized, orderly surrounding imparts a certain serenity. There is comfort in knowing that things are in their proper places. An organized individual often commands more respect and wields more power. He or she appears smarter, more controlled, and more confident. By running our lives in an orderly manner we waste less. Time, energy and material goods are conserved when our projects are planned and our plans are followed.

Clearly, the benefits provide incentive to become organized!

There are pitfalls, however. Many of us fall victim to the belief that if a little organization will improve our lives, complete organization will rocket us to the pinnacle of success. There are those who would urge us to map out entire years of our lives at a time—setting goals, deciding our activities, and adhering relentlessly to our schedules. The danger, of course, lies in a loss of perspective.

When each day is planned in precisely timed increments and depends upon the successful completion of the day preceding it, the monkey wrench of circumstance can easily shut down the whole operation.

And, just as the unorganized person suffers the stress of diminished achievement, so too does the organized individual bear stress. It may, in fact be far greater for those who attempt to work, eat, and even sleep according to plan.

Perhaps there is a middle ground. Perhaps we can become semi-organized so that we accomplish our tasks and still enjoy some unfettered free time. Perhaps we can live more effectively if organization is more loosely defined. For example, in an office, organization could mean knowing where to find your notes, your pen, and the phone before the fifth ring.

At home with small children, organization might mean keeping stairways clear of toys. And at home with older kids, organization might simply entail keeping a spot cleared on the table so there is some place to eat supper.

Happiness Creators

Some people pursue happiness; others create it. Happiness seekers, which most of us are, look for ways to make life easier, more interesting and more meaningful. We focus inwardly as we respond to life's opportunities and situations, gauging every happening by how well it gratifies our desires and satisfies our needs.

We hunger for an elusive something that will make us truly happy once and for all. Involved in our introspection, we sometimes neglect the needs and desires of people around us.

Happiness creators, by contrast, seem somehow innocent of self-needs. They approach life as an adventure, a thing to be experienced and enjoyed without putting demands on it. Such people consistently respond to others with a smile, a laugh, or a handshake. They are interested in everything from people and politics to sniglets and beer. They make the best of friends, for they listen with care and respond with sincerity.

Happiness creators have problems just like everyone else, but they refuse to allow their problems to destroy their enjoyment of life. They are people-oriented and happiest when they can help others to appreciate the wonders of life.

Happiness creators pursue wisdom and understanding throughout life. And even though they may never park their rewards in a three-car garage or drape them over their bodies, their happiness is of such richness and depth that it compels them to share it with the rest of us.

How to Deal with Scary People

It's Halloween time and that means a celebration of all things scary. Ghosts and goblins decorate neighborhoods. Carved pumpkins glow eerily with the light of stumpy candles hidden inside. Trick or treat outings yield bagsful of goodies. It's a deliciously creepy time when night falls earlier, setting the stage for spooky stories and frightful costumes.

Back at the workplace, scary characters know no season and they don't crawl back into their dens or under the bridge after Halloween is over. Trolls and witches walk among us every day, exercising their mischief and unleashing dark natures.

There are the rude and self-centered, who rarely notice you unless you interrupt their day. If you have no reason to interact with them, your best bet is to leave them alone. If you must interact, stay focused on the task at hand. Be prepared to endure some childish behavior but don't react to it.

There are the perpetually grumpy, who seem bent on sharing their gloom with everyone. While these people can be annoying and wearisome, they are harmless enough. They, too, are best left alone. More than that, if you can stay out of their way, your life will be sunnier. Don't try to cheer them up, they will only make fun of your rose-colored glasses.

Then there are those who seem to be purposefully mean, like the woman who drops snide comments about your clothes or hair or shoes as she struts around the office. Her haughty air and outrageous remarks make her hard to ignore. She is hard to confront, too, because most people are afraid of what she would say or do to a challenger. Therein lies the source of her mean power. She intimidates others.

This persona takes many forms. It can be a co-worker who pokes fun at your work or calls attention to your mistakes. It can be someone from another department who accuses your department of making their work late. It can be a boss who is never satisfied or who changes the priorities of your work daily.

These people are scary because they are so hard to argue with or to change. Don't try! You will only provide a target for their meanness. Recognize that although these people are difficult, they can only scare you if you allow them to.

If they point out your mistakes, thank them for the correction. If they make fun of you, smile and walk away. If they tell lies, like the one who blames your department for her failures, provide truthful information to people who need to know it.

The point of this advice is to help you get beyond the bad behavior of others to work on the best of your own. Whenever you deal with scary people, you need to remember that they are acting out of some inner motivation that has little if anything to do with you. Do not take it personally, do not accept it as your problem, and do not add fuel to whatever fires they like to start.

Watch these people interact with others and you will soon see that they treat most everyone the same. Rude behavior becomes habitual. It also tends to limit the places you can go and the people who will interact with you. Rude people have very small circles of friends and whatever influence they have is short lived.

Whenever you encounter scary people, always be the person you want to be, the one who makes you proud of yourself. This will take great self-discipline sometimes and you will undoubtedly react negatively from time to time. Forgive yourself and keep moving.

And remember this: We all have bad days. We live in scary times filled with pressure. We don't always respond very gracefully. But stay focused on your goals and do your best each day. Then even the creepiest of office ghouls won't scare you.

Imagine Your Power!

Ours is a troubled world. Problems and hardships of all descriptions create worry, doubt, fear and uncertainty within us and sometimes lead to depression. Much of our discomfort is the result of our thinking and attitudes.

A case in point: Recently we had a day of brilliant blue skies, picture-perfect sparkling white clouds and disappearing snow. The day was a visual definition of cheerfulness. But it was windy. Everywhere, people were complaining of the wind and the resulting "bitter" cold. They noticed the sunshine, yes, but continued to harp on that darn cold wind.

Isn't it so often true that we focus on the negative things around us or about us instead of concentrating on the good? When we think about self-improvement, we pinpoint our areas of deficiency and temporarily forget about what we already do well. Consistently well, at that.

How much time, for example, do you spend thinking about how others have disappointed you or how you have disappointed others? Our regrets and remorse can become considerable.

How often do you wonder about the meaning and purpose of your life? About what contribution you are making and what purpose you are serving? I have wondered the same, myself. Often. And I believe these are good questions to grapple with, provided we keep a sense of perspective.

I went for a walk on that windy, bitter cold day I mentioned earlier, and I was surprised to hear the gurgling of a stream. I asked myself, "What good is a stream? What purpose does it serve?"

Now I'm sure there are numerous environmentalists who could tell me precisely what a stream is worth. But realistically, that one small stream is not crucial to the well-being of my community. Funny thing, though. The stream made me happy. I stopped, listened, and appreciated that nondescript stream. Here was energy. Here was action. Here was a volume of water flowing freely, strongly, determinately toward its destination. To me, it represented commerce, enthusiasm.... Springtime? I was strangely uplifted.

Friends, if a stream can do this, just imagine the hundreds, no thousands, of ways you have made other people happy. Imagine what your presence has meant to someone, or your smile or the sound of your voice. As a unique individual among billions, you are absolutely irreplaceable. And very precious.

A bubbling stream and brilliant sunshine made me breathe deeply and smile despite cold and gusty winds. Imagine how much you have meant to others just because of who you are.

Lost!

ave you ever noticed how often we get lost? By "we" I mean mankind, womankind, all of us, each of us. Sometimes it seems we are lost all the time. We get lost in thought, lost in a fog, lost at sea and lost in space. We have long-lost friends. And we've all experienced to some degree the situation that is lost, hopeless and beyond remedy.

There are many ways to get lost and just as many reasons. The thing that is so frustrating is that we try so hard to keep our lives ordered and on track. We may prepare a master plan, schedule daily activities and write ourselves reminder notes. Invariably, the notes get lost and so, too, do we.

After a while, getting lost can begin to shake a person's self-confidence. You can begin to question your motives, your methods and occasionally your sanity. It can be particularly disconcerting when, after charting a careful course, you find that the world around you has changed. Your plans are shot. You are lost.

It's a frightening feeling. It yanks the solid earth out from under your feet leaving you lost in space. It takes the wind out of your sails leaving you lost at sea. It leaves you asking, "What now" while a giant lump of fear answers back, "I have no idea."

When we get lost, we lose sight of what is real. Our perspective is clouded over by fear and frustration and we are unable to find a solid grounding. Here is a silly suggestion that can work psychological magic. Tape a 3 x 5-inch index card to your bathroom mirror. Make a large red X on it and print the words, "You Are Here."

Look closely at that card each day and at your face in the mirror. Then remember:

- Despite any misfortunes, setbacks or lost opportunities, you are (still) here.

- While the world rages and storms around you, right now in this quiet space, you are (still) here.

- When you are not sure where you came from and have no idea where you are going, you can at least know for certain that *You Are Here.*

Roadmaps, careful plans, and good intentions can all get you lost. Being lost is a fact of life. By accepting it with good humor, common sense, and a sense of perspective, you can keep your wits about you and find ways to move forward again.

Menopause –
It Almost Took Me Down

*M*enopause is often called "the silent passage," and until recently it was one of those things you didn't talk about, even among friends. But as women of the Baby Boom generation began making the passage, all kinds of information became available on the science and psychology of this life change.

Menopause, The Musical debuted in Orlando, FL in 2001, blowing the lid off the silent passage and drawing women in huge numbers to dance, sing, and laugh at the maladies associated with menopause.

How far we've come.

I remember when I was in eighth grade, the mother of one of my best friends had a nervous breakdown. People shook their heads sadly and said it was because of "The Change," but that's all that was said about it. I wondered then what could possibly be so awful about any change that it would make a woman lose her mind.

Fast forward several decades. Now I get it.

The physical symptoms are well documented and oh so true. The body dries out and starts to sag, thanks to a redistribution of hormones.

It smolders like a moody teenager and erupts in flames at the most inopportune times. The brain fuzzes over, clouding the memory and sabotaging any ability to concentrate. Restful sleep is often hijacked first by the internal volcano, then by the icy shivers that follow.

When I see a winning coach get doused with Gatorade at the end of a football game, I sometimes think, "Try that every night for a couple of years and see how you feel."

That's my grumpy side, which was really quite foreign to me until a few years ago. I am an optimist. I like finding the good in things and letting others see it, too.

Which is probably why I am also a bit of a naturalist as far as treatment of health symptoms is concerned. Believing in the body's ability to regulate and right itself, I prefer to let it sort things out on its own. Menopause made a mockery of my stoic and patient nature.

The scariest part of menopause—and the aspect that almost took me down—is what it does to a woman's confidence. When the body no longer responds to diet or exercise the way it used to, when sleep is disturbed on a regular basis, and when the mind refuses to focus or function as it once did, self-confidence takes a hit.

When this happens, a woman may begin to do things that in stronger days she would not consider. Some women shop. Some stray. Some become fitness addicts. Some sip. A glass of wine while making dinner; one more to savor with the meal. Later, a cocktail before bed. And maybe one more to assure sleep. The well documented uptick in alcoholism among middle-aged women may have a link to menopause.

All these behaviors can make a woman feel like a stranger to herself, which worsens the sense of imbalance and anxiety. Most women tend to keep such troubled thoughts to themselves. They reason that no one would understand exactly what they're feeling, and besides, they'll soon get past this rough patch.

But the silent passage can last a long time. The damage done to a woman's confidence can lead to a gradual withdrawal from life and sometimes deep depression. That's what happened to my friend's mother so long ago. It is what threatened me so recently.

Ladies, do not succumb!

As with any difficult change, remember that your life so far has woven itself into a story complete with ups and downs, trials and triumphs. Be proud of where you've been and excited about where you're going. Don't try to wade through menopause on your own. It is a natural stage of life, and a challenging one. Stay socially active. Get involved in activities that bring you satisfaction. Have fun with your family. Refuse to give up your self-confidence!

This world needs all the talent, wisdom, and energy you can lend it. Preserve your health and your humor, trusting that a saner, happier, flash-free future is on its way!

Ode to Maturity

Maturity is a quality we admire in others and strive for ourselves. But what is maturity? The dictionary defines maturity as being fully grown or developed, ripened, or perfect and complete. This definition implies that there is no further growth or development possible and that after maturity comes an inevitable decline.

In a technical sense, we know this is true of fruits and vegetables. We eat them at the peak of their maturity before they begin to spoil. But this particular definition of maturity is not applicable to you and me. Who would want to become mature if it meant the end of growth and development?

The fact is that for each of us the opportunity for growth is present in every single new day. Each new thing we see, hear or learn affects the way we think. It changes us subtly and it is this change that provides evidence of growth.

Let's consider then, a different definition of maturity to apply to people. We might say maturity is a kind of serenity, an ability to deal with life's trials with a certain equilibrium. Maturity might mean the ability to accept those things in life that we are powerless to change. It might mean a greater tolerance for people and ideas that are different from our own. We could say that maturity is all these things. But let's add one more facet to the definition. Maturity is the ability and willingness to accept responsibility for what we say and do.

This sounds fairly simple, but think of the people you know, both young and old, whose favorite hobby is finding excuses. Everyone knows of the young student who fails to turn in an assignment on time and says, "The dog ate it." Two young children caught fighting can be expected to point to one another and say, "He started it." And every parent has raised a child whose favorite response to incriminating questions was a shrug of the shoulders or a mumbled, "I don't know."

These are responses we expect from children because they are immature. But most of us know immature older people as well. Typical phrases from these people might include, "I never got the message." "Harry screwed up." "I didn't say that," and yes, "He started it."

There are countless ways to avoid responsibility for our actions. Most of us have one or two favorites that we resort to in times of stress or fatigue. But remember that mature individuals—those who are generally serene, self-composed and tolerant—have little use for such excuses. Because they accept responsibility for their actions, they have no need for them.

One final thought: Mature individuals understand and accept the fact that they will never be fully ripened, complete and perfect. Happily, they just continue to grow and develop, finding joy and excitement in each new day.

Perfectionism, Circa 1984

"You demand perfection in yourself—mistakes are taboo, failure is worse than death, and even negative emotions are a disaster. You're supposed to look, feel, think and behave superbly at all times. Although you drive yourself at an intense pace, your satisfactions are meager. Once you do achieve a goal, another more distant goal instantly replaces it, so you never experience the reward of getting to the top of the mountain. Eventually you begin to wonder why the promised payoff from all your efforts never seems to materialize. Your life becomes a joyless, tedious treadmill. You are living with unrealistic, impossible personal standards, and you need to re-evaluate them."

Does this sound like you? It is a description of a perfectionist written by Dr. David D. Burns in his book *Feeling Good, The New Mood Therapy*. Perfectionism seems to be on the rise as people everywhere are striving to be the best at everything they do. Maybe this comes from a fear of missing out on the good things in life. We know that competition is fierce for jobs, for money and for mates; we've recently learned that the coming of age of the Baby Boomers has aggravated this situation.

We want to make sure we get our piece of the pie. On the other hand, a growing perfectionism may be the result of an innocent self-improvement kick that's gone haywire. No longer does a little self-improvement make the grade. Suddenly we feel we must come out Number One or our efforts have been wasted. The pressures mount tremendously when we feel that nothing but the best is acceptable and there is no room for error. Dr. Burns encourages us to challenge this attitude.

"Never give up your capacity for being wrong because then you lose the ability to move forward. In fact, just think what it would be like if you would be completely void of challenge and the satisfaction that comes from mastering something that takes effort. It would be like going to kindergarten for the rest of your life. You'd know all the answers and win every game. Every project would be a guaranteed success because you would do everything correctly. People's conversations would offer you nothing because you'd already know it all."

Maybe it's time we convince ourselves that practice does not have to make perfect.

Q-Tip as Diplomat

*H*ave you ever looked closely at a Q-Tip? Of course not. It's nothing more than an incidental part of our grooming habits.

Well, I've noticed something about Q-Tips that could pertain to people. In fact, if people would try to be a little more like Q-Tips, our coexistence might be more pleasant. It's not the job Q-Tips do that primarily interests me; it's how they are made. Q-Tips are soft at the contact points and sturdy in between.

Those characteristics describe in a nutshell the essence of diplomacy. For a Q-Tip, soft at the contact point means lots of cotton. For a person, a diplomat, it means handling human contact with sensitivity, patience, tolerance and attentiveness. It doesn't mean being a pushover, but it does imply cooperation. And for a Q-Tip to be sturdy in between, it requires a strong stick. For a person, it requires a strong character—a backbone—comprised of principles, ideals and lots of self-confidence.

Now, just as a Q-Tip is useless if it is pulled apart, so too is the idea of diplomacy if it is made up only of lots of cotton or strong sticks. It is the combination of these two ingredients and the counter balance created by them that is so effective. With strong beliefs and adequate self-confidence, we as diplomats find the security necessary to handle human contact graciously. We have no fear of being trod upon by others, but we have no need to strong-arm them, either. Toughness alone, we know, will serve to irritate and is likely to produce greater difficulty.

If, however, we are cotton through and through, we certainly will not harm anyone else, but we may end up big fluff balls with no ideas, no beliefs, and ultimately no respect. We know how easy it is to toss cotton aside.

So there it is: The humble Q-Tip standing as a symbol of diplomacy. The analogy is fitting, especially when you consider the purpose of each. A Q-Tip gently cleans out the junk to assure proper functioning of an organ. Isn't that the aim of diplomacy also?

Realistically Speaking

We often hear the statement, "Everyone wants to be a winner," but realistically, we know this is just not so. If everyone wanted to be a winner, everyone would jump out of bed at the crack of dawn and work mightily every minute of the day toward his particular goal. Everyone would be determined, energetic, single-minded, and persistent in his efforts.

Such behavior would, of course, point to the fact that everyone would have a goal. Realistically speaking, everyone should have a goal. Do you? Why do you get out of bed each day? Why do you work? Why do you pay attention to some things and not others? Why do you belong to certain groups and not others? What things do you look forward to in your life? What do you want to be? Do you want to amass wealth, contribute to society, gain fame? What is your goal?

For many of us these questions are difficult to answer. We shrug, squirm, chuckle and go on to more important things like what needs to be done tomorrow. Each of us, however, whether we are a realist or optimist, must answer the same fundamental questions of life: Who am I? What do I want? What can I do to get it? What does it mean?

Each of us has a different perspective; we come up with different answers. The optimist sees promise and challenge in life. He works hard toward his goals, even though to others they may seem unattainable. He believes the outcome will be worth his effort. He appreciates the inconsistencies of life and finds humor in them. Some take the optimist to be a fool.

The realist sees challenge in life, too. He, however, carefully measures the requirements and analyzes his skills. He rarely overestimates his capabilities and thus does not expend time or energy working toward something that is not likely to happen. He not only accepts the stumbling blocks of life, he expects them and handles them accordingly. People often admire the realist for his efficiency and practicality.

Realistically speaking, we could get along in life just fine by thinking logically, limiting our expectations and accepting things as they are. Positively speaking, that's not enough. The human spirit is irrepressible. It seeks, it strives, it rejoices. To the realist, this can be a source of discomfort and an irritant. To the optimist, it is the source of life. A positive attitude can—and does—make the difference between a life that is acceptable and one that is a joy.

The Christmas Crisis

t happens every year. Sometime between December 23 and December 25, a major Christmas crisis arises. You put off buying a gift for your spouse because you we looking for just the right thing and now store shelves are bare. The Christmas tree tips over, thanks to the kids or the dog, shattering half the ornaments. The hors d'oeuvres you made for your Christmas party flopped and guests are at the door. You are out of wrapping paper or tape at midnight Christmas Eve with six more gifts to wrap. One of the kids discovers that there is no Santa Claus, and the string of lights around the window outside breaks free and flaps in the breeze. Christmas once again has become unmanageable.

It's not an accident, you know. The heightened anticipation and tension of the holidays turn minor things into monumental catastrophes. A general slowdown of pace and a different perspective will help solve the Christmas crisis.

For the special person about whom you procrastinated, pick a small favorite something, be it candy, a magazine, or movie tickets. Give this gift on Christmas. Then plan together a special weekend getaway or other out-of-the-ordinary event. The gift of time is precious.

When the tree takes a tumble, catch the expression on the kids' faces. Their innocent shock and horror can be humorous if you manage to stay calm. Empathize a little bit. They honestly feel worse than you do.

Don't worry about flopped hors d'oeuvres; simple food like cheese and crackers, fruit or nuts will suffice. Provide an abundance of warmth and good cheer for your guests and your party will be delightful. Substitute newspaper (the comic section is particularly good) for wrapping paper and string or glue for tape. If all else fails, pull out socks and make your gifts oversized stocking stuffers. Or hide the gifts and make the recipient hunt for them. Improvise!

When the kids give up Santa, they are ready to learn about love and sharing among family members. Now is the time to emphasize that cost does not determine value. Remind your children that it is the thought that counts.

Finally, lights will fall down; they will malfunction. Spotlights will short-circuit and wreaths will hang crooked. That's Christmas! Relax and enjoy the holidays, concentrating on the little pleasures and sudden joys while downplaying the aggravations. Just think of all the family stories you are creating.

Time for a Change

ey look! It's another New Year! Another chance to build that fantastic future you've been thinking about! Aren't you excited?

Perhaps after a year like last year, you feel some skepticism. You may wonder how much more stamina, optimism, and sheer survival you'll need to succeed.

The month of January often finds us thinking a little schizophrenically. On one hand we're excited about what lies ahead and we hope the New Year will roll in like a shiny new penny. On the other hand, we remember too many New Years past that started with a bang and ended with a whimper. We fear that this New Year might roll over us like a dark heavy cloud. One minute we're up, the next minute we're down and pretty soon we're worn out even before we start doing anything.

What's a woman to do? Make New Year's Resolutions! Call upon your deepest desires and buck up your sturdiest resolve! Surely this is Your Year!

And it may well be. But when you're already stressed, tired, and worried, you may wonder how setting even bigger goals will help?

Let's pause to recognize that over the years many of us have been programmed to focus on performance, to do our best—To make a difference!—and to make a pile of money in the process. The New Year's Resolution strategy fits this programming.

But what if you were to take a different approach? What if you were to ask yourself, "What do I value about my life that I want to maintain in the coming year?" What if, instead of seeking quantum leap improvement, you sought to protect something precious?

Suppose your answer is "My health." Now you have a different proposition. Instead of making promises about weight loss and daily workouts, you can brainstorm little ways to maintain your health. These might include eating better and getting more exercise, but they might also include reading uplifting material, hanging around with positive, successful people, and talking about building things rather than surviving hardship. These are ideas that appeal. None of them requires a gym membership, a major time commitment, or venturing out into the cold. Maybe, just maybe, you can begin to improve your outlook by maintaining something that is important to you—your health.

What if you also kept track of the ways you take care of your health each day? Simple notes in a daily journal create evidence of your caretaking and progress. This might cause you to see how effective you can be at making yourself happy. And maybe this happier, more effective you will start to attract a new kind of attention that opens up new opportunities. Gradually, in a quiet and private way, you begin to change your life while taking good care of yourself.

I am reminded of a photo I saw recently of a bald-headed woman. A cancer survivor. Her story is one of persistence, belief, and gratitude, as is the case for a growing number of women we know.

What struck me about this particular photo was the look in the woman's eyes. Her gaze was steady, her eyes clear. There was a sense of great wisdom that shone from her eyes, as though she knows we can't really understand her story unless we, too, have been there. But it doesn't matter. She is powerful in her serenity as she encourages women to take care of their health, to seek goodness, and to have patience and hope and faith in a new day.

These are quintessential messages that women have offered for generations. It is what we teach our children when they have a bad day at school or suffer a heart-breaking loss on the athletic field. It is the counsel we offer friends struggling with big decisions or deep disappointment. "Tomorrow will come. Your heart will heal. You will do something exceptional in time." It is a quiet message of truth, steeped in experience.

Season of the Second Chance

S pring is almost as fraught with clichés about new beginnings and fresh starts as New Year's. But considering that it follows New Year's Eve by almost three months, spring might more aptly be called the season of the second chance.

Remember your New Year's Eve resolution to lose ten pounds? Those ten pounds are now 15 and spring is the time to get serious about losing them. How about your resolution to spend more time with the family? You may have been in close physical proximity throughout the winter, but each family member was probably in his or her own cocoon. Spring provides the chance to be together outdoors—to go for walks or wash the car or fly kites.

New Year's resolutions are made in the midst of a cold, blustery, gray season. Our springtime resolve comes with the re-awakening of life. Brighter mornings, longer days and new color all around help to quicken our responses to life. We shed the heaviness of winter and move toward the lightness and openness of spring.

Yes, spring truly is the season of the second chance. This is significant, for if nature provides a way for us to make good on past resolutions, perhaps we should do likewise. Too often an incorrect choice, an unfortunate circumstance, a failure in one area of life spells doom and gloom in other areas. This need not be so if we can accept the essence of spring into our lives. We can learn to view past mistakes as unfulfilled New Year's resolutions that were made with good intentions.

By adopting a fresh, spring-like attitude, we come to realize that every moment holds the potential for new beginnings. We can have faith in the promise of tomorrow just as we find joy in the promise of spring.

Spring Beats Winter Every Time

Spring is battling winter for control of the seasons and for us it is a frustrating struggle. One day we have sunshine and moderate temperatures; the next day brings clouds, drizzle, snow flurries or a biting wind. Yet with each turn of the calendar page, we become more tolerant and optimistic for we know that winter is staging its last few squalls.

The struggle between spring and winter can be compared to our struggle to improve ourselves and to solve tough problems. The changing of the season does not come without turmoil, nor does it happen on the prescribed calendar day. The process is gradual and often erratic. Remember that gorgeous day in February when everyone thought spring would be early this year? Winter managed to fight back so that now, in mid-March, we still see sizable snow piles. But we know that soon winter will disappear. We know it and we believe it.

Yet, what happens when we try to eliminate a habit we would rather not have? The first thing we do is get very firm with ourselves. We vow, "No more." Then we think about little else until our resistance breaks down and we slide back into the old habit. The second thing we generally do is decide that we didn't really want to change in the first place. And we usually feel disappointed.

Of course, this scenario does not always occur within the first few days of our efforts. Sometimes it happens after several weeks' worth of trying. Unfortunately, however, many of us fail to recognize that despite the starts and stops, the success and setbacks of our projects, if we would only stick with them long enough, we would achieve our goals. Just as spring does not come overnight, neither do our goals become instant realities.

We need to learn patience. We need to learn persistence. Most importantly, we need to learn to relax and trust ourselves to succeed. The only way to do this, of course, is through consistent effort. Despite our stumbles and falls, we can get up and go on. Think of all the battles spring loses to winter. But eventually, spring wins. You can, too.

Three Wishes

I have learned to seek my happiness by limiting my desires,
rather than in attempting to satisfy them.
　　　　　　　　　—John Stuart Mill

C an you imagine anyone you know saying that? Who, in our time, would conceive of limiting desires instead of feverishly trying to satisfy every desire imaginable? The media, your neighbor, your best friend, and your big shot brother-in-law tell you to go for it. Do more, get more, be more are the messages we hear every day. Most of the world races frantically to satisfy first one desire, then another.

Fast trackers, for instance, get all the attention. Their lifestyles intrigue the less active; their possessions are the envy of many. Yet researchers are finding that fast-trackers are increasingly unhappy. Despite all their accomplishments and accouterments they hunger for more meaning and more fulfillment.

What wisdom we find then in Mr. Mill's comment. The message is clearly stated, but difficult to absorb and act upon. Limit your desires and satisfy them well. One cannot help but find happiness in such satisfaction. Happiness, serenity, and indeed the strength to resist the clamor around us that encourages us—no, convinces us—to desire more and to chase after more.

Try this little exercise. If you could have three wishes, what would they be? Keep in mind that three wishes is the limit. You may not use one wish to wish for more. This is a child's game, but try it anyway. What three things are most important to you? Can you single them out? Write them down. Study them. Reflect on the consequences of obtaining these three things. How would your life change? How would these wishes enhance or alter the relationships you have with others? How would these wishes enhance or alter your own self-perception?

After answering these questions, you may find that one or more of your three initial wishes are not worth achieving. In that case, you'd better start over.

This silly exercise can be used seriously to decide what your priorities are in life. Use it when you feel torn in too many directions, when you ache for too many unrealized dreams. To limit our desires is not to deny ourselves the good things in life. Rather it is to reach an emotional maturity that will aid us in becoming stronger, more effective, and happier individuals.

To be Human is to Complain!

ankind is the only species on earth that has the ability to complain with eloquence about nearly everything. We complain about being too hot or too cold, too tall or too short, too fat or too thin. We complain about not being smart enough or about being overqualified. Our shoes pinch, our roofs leak, our kids don't mind and our spouses don't talk. We have too much to do with too little help in too little time.

There are two things about complaining that deserve some thought. First, if we were to take all our complaints and look at them as a whole, we would have to chuckle at the fact that we complain about being human.

Do dogs complain about their weight? Do fish complain about being too hot or too cold? Do trees complain about property taxes? Of course not. Which of these or the millions of other things in the world would you rather be?

Second, what do things you complain about tell about the things you already have? For instance, a lot of people complain about not being able to stick to a diet and lose weight. This means more than that their bellies are literally and figuratively full. They have the means to buy food. They have the equipment needed to prepare it. They have the freedom to choose what they will and will not eat. They are healthy enough to ingest and digest foods they choose to eat.

The fact is that most of us are safe and secure enough in our homes, our places of work and our country to be freed from concerns over survival, punishment and the many other terrors known to less fortunate humans. In short, by looking at the nature of our complaints we can backtrack to see just how many other needs and wants have already been satisfied.

Will our complaining ever cease? Probably not. The better things get in our personal worlds, the more perfect we like to envision them. But the higher our level of complaining, the more fulfilled we are in the basics of life. Let's make a mental checklist of all the things we don't have to complain about. Such a practice will foster appreciation. It may also cut down on the number of complaints we have.

Trust Your Gut!

Common sense—good, old-fashioned horse sense—is a much-needed commodity in today's world of experts and specialists. Specialists everywhere provide solutions to problems that most of us haven't thought of yet. And experts show us how to achieve everything from overnight fame and fortune to instant self-understanding and beautiful relationships.

What makes us trust the expert or the specialist more than our own experience, intuition, or gut feeling? Has society made us so insecure that we trust only those who occupy privileged positions with regard to knowledge, experience or advanced degrees? We have been led to believe that run-of-the-mill citizens do not have the necessary tools to make the best decisions. Because the world is changing so rapidly and new information is constantly surfacing, popular opinion holds that we are obliged to pay heed to those who dedicate their lives to a particular field of study.

Pay heed, yes, of course. But capitulate? Be careful.

It is true that some problems, and particularly those that pose severe consequences, must be dealt with by individuals and institutions that are most qualified to handle them. For instance, if something was physically wrong with a specific organ or system of my body that was beyond the experience of a general practitioner, I would want a specialist's opinion.

However, and this is a big however, nothing exists in a vacuum. We must understand that because everything is interrelated, the treatment of one ill will affect other areas that may or may not also require treatment.

Sometimes a specialist—medical or otherwise—becomes so absorbed in a problem or role or function that he or she is blinded to other interrelated factors. The ethical implications of genetic engineering is an example. (And it's only an example.) While the good of one area may be served, the overall good could be impaired; and while the solution to one problem may be found (a particular illness genetically eliminated), other unforeseen problems (elimination of fetuses carrying defective genetic coding) could be created. It's the law of unintended consequences at work. Just because we can do something, doesn't mean we should.

Common sense, folks! You can't live without it. Take the advice of experts with a grain of salt. Compare it to what you know to be true. Consult your innards and others you respect. Don't be bullied through life by those who claim to be richer in knowledge or longer on experience. After all, in the final analysis, who can know what's better for you than you?

What If You Were Born Perfect?

*T*his might seem like a silly question and indeed it may suggest a radical thought. But what if you were born perfect? What if you arrived on this planet equipped in every way that mattered to live the life only you could live? What if the circumstances, events, and people that have crossed your path thus far were precisely right for you? What if the mistakes you made came at exactly the right time to be of maximum instructional benefit? What if all the things you have acquired came into your life at just the right moment and all the things you have discarded or lost left your world at a similarly just-right moment?

Imagine how happy you would be if all this were true. Guess what? It is.

Advertisers the world over work hard to help you believe that if only you had flawless skin, a sculpted body, beautiful home, the coolest technologies, pitch-perfect voice, a partner who turns heads, and diamonds on your right hand, you would (finally) be completely happy.

The beauty of this storyline for them is that while you may have one or several of these fortunate assets, chances are slim you have them all. So there is always something to work on, wish for, and be ever so slightly unhappy about. Discontent fuels sales. And makes you and me fantastic target markets.

Consider these numbers. A woman in the US spends $1,035 each year on cosmetics. Let's use $20 as an average cost per cosmetic. That's high for some items, low for others, but as an average probably about right. At $20 per cosmetic, a woman purchases roughly 52 items each year.

When it comes to weight loss, the numbers are even more remarkable. The global market for weight loss products is $222 BILLION annually. In the US, 80 million people buy weight loss products each year. That's a lot of people spending a lot of money to change fundamental aspects of themselves.

Let's try on a different idea. Let's imagine you are, right now, just the way you should be.

Your shortfalls are necessary in order for your strengths to be apparent. Your physical quirks are unique marks of distinction, like Brook Shields' eyebrows, Cindy Crawford's mole or Queen Latifah's size. Why are these traits considered adorable for these women but horrendous for you? [Hint: Acceptance creates beauty.]

The worldview you have developed as a result of many experiences resides behind your eyes only. No one has been where you have been, or seen, heard, or learned what you have. Nobody puts thoughts together in exactly the same way you do.

This is something to be embraced and quietly celebrated. Your perspective is unique and interesting. Yet many women—maybe even you—spend great amounts of time cataloging all the things that are not quite right about them.

The tendency to compare oneself to others is normal. And yes, there is always room for improvement. But when you look to those who seem better off in terms of finances, beauty, or material possessions, you get a skewed view of life and its rewards.

From a practical standpoint, you not only waste time and precious energy feeling sad or worried or frustrated, you lose the time and opportunity to develop the gifts you do have and to make a difference that only you can make.

Tune into Bruno Mars' song, *Just The Way You Are*. It is a sweet song by a young artist crooning about a youthful beauty. He tells an important truth that gets truer with age. "When you smile, the whole world stops and stares for a while, 'cause, Girl, you're amazing, just the way you are." (WE NEED TO REQUEST PERMISSION TO USE THE LYRICS …)

Indeed.

Wisdom from Ben Franklin

Clichés are bad news. They're old, stale, and boring. Usually whatever they say is so old-fashioned that they have no relevance at all. Most of them anyway.

Ben Franklin was a cliché maker. He was also a brilliant inventor, a prominent politician (in those days that was an OK thing to be), and many considered him a genius. Perhaps he was just blessed with an extraordinary amount of common sense.

At any rate, here are some of Ben's rules for behavior, a few of which have become modern-day clichés. I've added some editorial comments—you can skip those if you want. But as you read, remember that in Ben's days, they didn't know you should "never say never."

- Never put off until tomorrow what you can do today. (Truly hackneyed, but wise nonetheless.)

- Never trouble another for what you can do yourself. (Self-sufficiency is a virtue, no?)

- Never spend your money before you have it. (Chuckle.)

- Never buy what you do not want because it is cheap. (Avoid rummage sales.)

- Pride costs us more than hunger, thirst, and cold. (Makes us look more foolish, too.)

- We seldom repent having eaten too little. (Pig out and suffer.)

- Nothing is troublesome that we do willingly. (Exercise is troublesome.)

- How much pain the evils have cost us that have never happened. (Don't worry, be happy.)

- Take things always by the smooth handle. (Splinters hurt?)

- When angry, count 10 before you speak; if very angry, a hundred. (Amen.)

And my personal favorite:

- Experience keeps a dear school, but fools can learn in no others and scarcely in that; for it is true, we may give advice, but we cannot give conduct. Remember this: they that will not be counseled cannot be helped. If you do not hear reason, she will rap you over your knuckles.

With Age Comes Wisdom

"You are wise beyond your years." We say this to young people who seem to have a way of understanding life and dealing with its vagaries that suggests they have lived longer than their actual age. If someone has said this to you, be happy. It was a compliment.

Years later, when gravity has pulled your body parts toward Mother Earth, your eyesight has dimmed, and your hearing has become a family joke, you may come to think of wisdom as a cosmic booby prize for enduring life. In truth, wisdom is a gift.

A wise woman knows the truth of the bumper sticker: "Aging is not for sissies!" It can be depressing sometimes. It requires a strong sense of self to transition from fresh-faced, bright-minded, and able-bodied to something else. We are challenged to adapt as our bodies change over time.

This can be confusing. Remember the awkward transition from innocent child to angst-ridden adolescent? You may have sailed right through it or you may have suffered mightily. Either way, you did get through it.

Your body is quite amazing in its natural ability to develop and mature. It is the mind that creates trouble. Maybe you are like some women who think they should be able to retain their youthful faces and figures forever, especially if you spend precious time, energy and money in this effort! Maybe you think your troubles should recede with time; that at a certain stage of life you should be comfortable, rewarded for years of effort. Maybe you think people should respect you more as the years pass, not less. These thoughts can lead to deep dissatisfaction. They can furrow your brow and push you toward comfort food and TV shows. Which of course create bodily evidence that aging is not your friend.

What if you could change your mind about all this? What if you could accept the fact that passing years bring changes to body and mind and that changing circumstances require new ideas and behaviors? Certainly the political and financial strife that surrounds us today is unsettling. Accepting reality and learning to live within its confines are signs of wisdom. We can learn. We can continue to grow. Most important, we can find happiness in the midst of pain.

This lesson has presented itself to me many times. One of the most poignant instances came years ago, when I thought I would be immune to the empty nest syndrome, that time of life when women suffer deep feelings of loss as their children leave home for good. I was a working, traveling mom and my daughters learned to be self-sufficient at an early age.

Still, we were very close while they were growing up, openly sharing our challenges and enjoying our plans. We had things to do in the world. How confused I was when my youngest departed the nest and I was left with uncomfortable questions of self-identity. My daughters had given me purpose my entire adult life. When they encamped on their own life adventures, I was left to ponder this purpose. I was genuinely surprised at how sad I felt and how paralyzed I was for a significant period of time.

The same feelings of sadness can arise as you notice sagging skin, startling wrinkles, and physical decline. None of these appear over-night, yet they seem stunning when you notice them. Wisdom is that quiet whisper that calls you to accept what is and embrace a new chapter of beauty.

To be a gorgeous woman at any age, start now. Move away from the mirror and out into the world. Be curious; an engaged mind brightens the eye. Help others; an extended hand strengthens the arm. Listen and laugh; a joyful heart softens the face.

A wise woman knows that when you approach life with an interest in learning, helping, and growing, happiness is multiplied and sorrow loses its sharpest sting. Maya Angelou, one of the wisest women of our time, reminds us that life loves to be taken by the lapel and told: "I'm with you, kid. Let's go."

Working Moms

or decades there's been an ongoing discussion, debate—okay argument—over whether women with small children should go to work or stay home to raise the family. "Should"—it's a stifling word.

Truth is, whether we work for hire or work at home, every woman with a family is a working mom.

Full disclosure: I was an outside-the-home, traveling, sometimes single working mom when my two daughters were growing up. I was a heavy user of daycare services. My younger sister, a stay-at-home mom, challenged me frequently about my choices, and made them into a moral challenge. "Why did you even have kids if you were going to allow someone else to raise them?"

That was more than thirty years ago, and the temperature around this debate has not subsided. So as we celebrate Mother's Day, I'd like to weigh in with some thoughts on motherhood, employment, and the well-being of children.

Motherhood and Employment

I grew up in a family of six kids. Mom stayed at home, chafing under the expectations of a traditional role, until my youngest brother entered kindergarten. Then she went back to school. I was outraged.

I thought her decision was selfish and that it was going to spell disaster for my brother. I told her so. Looking back, I respect both her courage and her fortitude in choosing her path against some noisy opposition. If I was outraged, Dad was furious!

Years later, my own decision to work full-time was born of economic necessity. I simply didn't have the option to stay home and this turned out to be a good thing. I was a happier woman and a more patient mother thanks to the stimulation and affirmation of the outside world. When I played with, fed, or listened to my daughters, I did so with curiosity and wonder because I was so tuned into them when we were together. I don't know that I'd have been so attentive if I'd been with them 24/7.

There's a popular expression today: "If Mama's not happy, nobody's happy." From personal experience, I must say, "No kidding."

Kids' Well-being

Kids need role models. They need boundaries. They need to know that while they are important and will be cared for, they are not the center of the universe for everyone at all times.

I believed that my primary job as a mom was to teach my kids how to deal effectively with a world gone crazy while being strong, optimistic, pragmatic, and compassionate. I also believed that the best way to teach was to model these qualities. I've kept a beautiful reminder taped to my refrigerator for more than thirty years. It's called *Children Learn What They Live* by Dorothy Law Nolte.

Trade-offs

Moms who go off to work each day encounter expectations at home and on the job that, combined, are often unreasonable. The pressure of being responsible for raising decent, well-adjusted children while maintaining a level of productivity on the job is enormous.

There's often a feeling of being only okay and never really great at one role or another. Fatigue is a given. Bad bosses make normal childhood issues seem worse. But the benefits are attractive: money, status outside the home, insurance, adult interaction.

How about the moms who work at home? A fact sheet might list these details: Hours: 24/7, no exceptions. No paid vacations, 401(k)s, expense accounts, or insurance. No overt recognition (or thanks) and no evidence of success until years down the line.

These working moms are expected at all times to be grateful for their 'easy' lives, happy as they serve their broods, and stunningly beautiful as they stand alongside successful spouses.

The downside: social isolation, feelings of irrelevance, intractable fatigue, and financial dependency. Are the expectations of at-home moms any more unreasonable than those placed on moms working outside the home?

Pick your poison, ladies.

And that's the problem. We look at our roles as working moms and see the poison of fatigue, unrealistic expectations, and missed opportunities. In our distraction, we miss the chance to be intentional role models for our kids, to see the dreams reflected in their innocent eyes, and to teach them how, little by little, they can become the people they most want to be. No job is more important.

And the truth is that the way you live teaches kids what they can expect from life. On this Mother's Day, take a few moments to realize that you are shaping the future. Congratulations, Mom. You matter.

Afterword

fter more than 30 years of working with people from all walks of life at various life stages, I am face to face with a new challenge—to build the Backbone Institute.

Across the US and indeed around the world, an epidemic loss of confidence has eroded all of our most important institutions: families, schools, churches, businesses, non-profit agencies, and governments. Failing schools have claimed headlines for too many years while businesses struggle to find qualified workers and entrepreneurs try to build new companies amid tighter credit terms and growing regulation. Competition for charitable donations threatens non-profits. Changing social mores challenge once-understood norms and political leaders lose trust with every broken promise.

At the foundation of so much disappointment lies a growing sense of personal vulnerability and despair. This is not new in the history of the world, but it is unfamiliar to current generations who have been largely raised during good economic times and promised a life of ease. Evidence of this is seen as "helicopter parents" continue to keep careful watch over children through college and early career stages. This watchfulness prevents developing adults from experiencing life's challenges and thus the ability to learn coping skills.

Movement away from rigorous grading systems in schools and a propensity to award effort rather than outcome, especially evident with sporting teams that favor universal participation over a winning record, are small examples that build to cumulatively weak confidence.

As generations of protected young people enter the workforce, they bring a marked inability to deal with the rough and tumble of an intensely competitive business world. At the same time, older generations of workers find their traditional values under assault even while technological advances push them to adapt more quickly to change. These are but a few examples of how confidence has been systematically, albeit unintentionally, damaged in recent years.

Given this erosion of personal and institutional confidence, there is an intense need to rebuild foundations. Backbone Institute will answer this need by teaching and fostering five fundamental skills: critical thinking, decisiveness, clarity of communication, integrity of word and act, and consistency. As mastery of these skills grows, confidence does, too. Fortified confidence enables intelligent, purposeful risk on behalf of individuals and the families, communities, and organizations they serve.

One of the unique offerings of Backbone Institute will be a series of Backbone Guides offering challenge, support, and inspiration to specific groups—women, young professionals, geeks, non-profit leaders, parents, and educators. Additionally, we will offer Confidence Clinics to these groups to strengthen the five skills and encourage individuals to make a difference in their circles of influence.

It is a big undertaking with no guarantee of success. I believe my life so far has been a learning laboratory that has equipped me—sometimes painfully—to do this work. I know there are partners waiting to be engaged. And I know we—you and me, wherever we are and however we engage—have been put here to make a difference. Let's get busy!

Backbone Guide Series:

Of Beauty and Substance: A Backbone Guide for Women
The Rise of Emerging Leaders: A Backbone Guide
for Young Professionals
Leveraging Your Genius: A Backbone Guide for Geeks
Minding the Social Fabric: A Backbone Guide
for Non-Profit Leaders
Raising the Future: A Backbone Guide for Parents
Empowering the Future: A Backbone Guide for Educators

Acknowledgments

*E*very story in this book calls to mind a special person or people who shaped the story and wove a thread into the fabric of my life. It would be impossible to name and thank them all. But here are some who have had a hand in outlining the design of the tapestry.

Mom, Dad, sisters Lynn and Lori, brothers Steve, Paul, and Dean. Thanks for the mischief we created and the friendships we formed. Grandma L., long gone, taught me to listen closely and make my own decisions. Extended family—aunts, uncles, cousins, nieces and nephews—taught me that despite family ties, we're all different. What a relief! Cousin Chris Witty, gold medal speed skater in the 2002 Olympics, thanks for showing us all how a champion grows up. What a thrill it was to watch you win in Salt Lake City!

There are countless others to thank for their role in shaping my thinking and expanding my view of the future. Elementary and high school friends, teachers, counselors, coaches. The nuns who rapped our knuckles and lay teachers who warned us to behave. Mrs. Mueller in third grade, Miss Stevens in fifth. Etaff...

People I met throughout a fragmented 13-year college career. Bani and Madhu Mahadeva, professors at the University of Wisconsin-Oshkosh. Chuck Vittorio, beloved compadre now departed. I'll never forget you guys.

Husbands who came and went. We struggled and hopefully learned from each other. Bosses—good, bad, and ugly—shaped my understanding of business and small-p politics.

My remarkable daughters, Jen and Kel, continue to teach and inspire me with their wit, wisdom, and genuine beauty. You know I love you for making me better every day we share. Their husbands, Scott and Steve—brothers!—take such pride in caring for their wives and families. Thank you for loving the girls. Granddaughters Peyton, Maya, Lilly, and Lexie remind me that sometimes children have a better grasp of what's important than adults. Thank you for your laughter and endless questions.

Marine Billy, LOML, shows me what true courage, dignity, honor, and respect look like in everyday life. It's not easy, but it certainly is worthwhile. Thank you for helping me grow up.

Church ladies Lois, Marlene, Joanne, Mary, and Betty. Your wisdom, sass, and support have lightened many a load and brightened many a day. Thank you for your love. You are precious to me.

Publisher Kira Henschel and graphic designer/web guru Elaine Meszaros, my thanks and special appreciation for making this book one that touches people with its grace. Your patience and persistence in this work and the upcoming Backbone Guide Series have given me sustenance during "those" days. You are powerful women.

Friends, colleagues, and clients too numerous to mention have shaped my thinking, touched my heart, and caused me to challenge my own assumptions. What blessings you have brought to my life. I thank every one of you.

Ultimate thanks, of course, to God the Father of us all. His magnificence is reflected in every one of His creations. His wisdom is profound. I recognize it every time I see how my mistakes turn out to be gifts in disguise. His unconditional love amazes me as it rises new every morning. His forgiveness makes me determined to do better. His grace makes life worth living.

About the Author

*F*or more than 20 years, Susan A. Marshall, President of Executive Advisor, LLC and Founder of Backbone Institute, has worked with senior leaders, leadership teams, and high potential professionals in business, education and non-profit organizations to strengthen executive skills and develop greater confidence as thinkers, planners, problem solvers and leaders.

For two years, as part of New York Mayor Bloomberg's school reforms, she worked with New York City public school principals, helping them overcome history and bureaucracy to assume responsibility for leadership in their schools. Similarly, working for more than 10 years as a colleague of University of Michigan professor Noel Tichy (author of *Judgment, The Leadership Engine, Control Your Destiny or Someone Else Will,* and many other leadership books) Susan worked with national senior leadership teams at Boys and Girls Clubs of America to transform club operations with a stronger focus on outcomes for children.

She traveled to Brunei in 2010 as part of Tichy's global team working with the Minister of Education to transform public education in the face of looming oil shortages and a need to develop a globally minded future workforce. A similar demand for dramatically improved student performance existed at two charter school systems in Texas, where Susan worked with leaders to elevate expectations, create partnerships with parents, and improve outcomes for a largely disadvantaged student population.

Susan has also led leadership workshops and provided executive coaching for C-suite leaders at some of the most recognized businesses in America, including GE, Apple, GM, and Harley-Davidson, as well as multinational private firms, start-up entities, and non-profit agencies. She wrote and taught an MBA leadership course for a private college in Milwaukee, Wisconsin, and has served as a mentor and advisor to hundreds of college students preparing to enter the workforce. Susan's work has touched more than 5,000 individuals and hundreds of executive teams. Add in conference speaking and this number doubles.

Marshall's book, *How to Grow a Backbone: 10 Strategies for Gaining Power and Influence at Work*, published in 2000 and translated into multiple languages, is gaining renewed interest as she speaks and teaches across the country.

This renewed interest stems from a growing need, as well as Susan's expanding reputation. It provides a powerful opportunity to advance and grow this work in a systematic way by building Backbone Institute.

Through workshops, books, podcasts, keynote addresses, facilitator training, personal coaching and online membership, Backbone Institute brings tested and proven development and accountability tools and techniques along with personal progress monitors to businesses, educational and non-profit institutions, and the wellness industry.

Susan welcomes your questions, comments, and suggestions via email at susan@backboneinstitute.com.